Java Made Simple

Master OOP, Build Cross-Platform Apps, and Ace Interviews

Booker Blunt

Rafael Sanders

Miguel Farmer

Boozman Richard

Chapter 1: Introduction to Java 9

What is Java? 9

History and Evolution of Java.................................... 11

Setting Up the Development Environment........................ 11

Writing and Running Your First "Hello, World!" Program........ 13

Key Java Concepts Overview 14

Hands-On Project: Create a "Hello, World!" Java Program 15

Conclusion 16

Chapter 2: Understanding the Java Syntax...................... 17

1. Variables, Data Types, and Constants........................ 18

2. Operators and Expressions...................................... 20

3. Control Flow Statements... 23

4. Hands-On Project: Build a Simple Calculator 25

Conclusion 26

Chapter 3: Mastering Object-Oriented Programming (OOP) in Java 28

1. The Basics of Object-Oriented Programming (OOP) in Java 29

The Four Key Principles of OOP: 30

2. The Difference Between Classes and Objects 31

3. Encapsulation 33

Hands-On Example: Build a Car Class with Encapsulation ... 33

4. Real-World Applications of Encapsulation.................... 37

Chapter 4: Inheritance and Polymorphism 40

1. What is Inheritance?... 41

2. Polymorphism: Method Overloading and Overriding 44

3. Hands-On Project: Extend the Car Class with Subclasses 47

4. Real-World Application: Using Polymorphism in a Payment System.. 50

Conclusion 52

Chapter 5: Abstraction and Interfaces 53

1. Abstract Classes vs. Interfaces 54

2. Key Differences Between Abstract Classes and Interfaces 57

3. Using Interfaces for Flexibility 58

4. Hands-On Project: Design a Payment Interface 58

Conclusion 62

Chapter 6: Working with Collections in Java 63

1. Introduction to Collections............................... 64

2. Common Interfaces: List, Set, Map....................... 65

3. Working with Lists, Sets, and Maps...................... 68

4. Hands-On Project: Build a Library Management System ... 72

5. Conclusion.. 75

Chapter 7: Exception Handling in Java 77

Introduction.. 77

1. Understanding Exceptions................................ 79

2. The try-catch-finally Block.............................. 81

3. Custom Exceptions 83

4. Hands-On Example: Build a Simple Banking Application .. 84

5. Best Practices in Exception Handling.................... 87

Conclusion 88

Chapter 8: Java Streams and Lambda Expressions 89

Introduction to Functional Programming in Java 89

1. The Power of Streams and Lambda Expressions in Modern Java.. 91

2. Working with Streams.. 92

3. Understanding the Stream Pipeline 94

4. Hands-On Example: Manipulate a List of Employees 95

5. Real-World Application: Data Analysis in Java 98

Conclusion 101

Chapter 9: Building Cross-Platform Apps with JavaFX 102

Introduction to JavaFX... 102

1. Understanding JavaFX: The Basics 103

2. Basic JavaFX Components.. 104

3. Hands-On Project: Build a To-Do List Application........... 109

4. JavaFX Advanced Features 112

Conclusion 115

Chapter 10: Developing Mobile Apps with Java (Android) 117

Introduction to Android Development with Java 117

1. Why Java is Still the Go-To Language for Android
Development 119

2. Setting Up Android Studio and Understanding Android
Components 120

3. Creating Your First Android App 122

4. Hands-On Example: Build a Basic Calculator App for
Android 124

5. Java Advanced Features in Android................................. 129

Conclusion 130

Chapter 11: Understanding Java Design Patterns 131

Introduction to Design Patterns.. 131

1. What Are Design Patterns? 132

2. Common Design Patterns and Their Use Cases 133

3. Hands-On Example: Build a Simple Logging System 140

4. Best Practices for Using Design Patterns in Real-World Projects 142

Conclusion 143

Chapter 12: Working with Databases in Java (JDBC) 144

Introduction to JDBC (Java Database Connectivity) 144

1. Understanding JDBC (Java Database Connectivity) 146

2. Setting Up JDBC and Connecting to a Database 147

3. CRUD Operations with JDBC 148

4. Hands-On Example: Build a Simple Inventory Management System 155

Conclusion 156

Chapter 13: Multithreading and Concurrency 157

Introduction to Multithreading and Concurrency 157

1. What is Multithreading? 159

2. Threads and the Runnable Interface 160

3. Managing Threads with Executor Service 162

4. Hands-On Example: Build a Simple File Downloader 164

5. Real-World Application: Enhancing Performance in Data Processing Systems 167

6. Conclusion 169

Chapter 14: Preparing for Java Interviews 170

Introduction 170

1. Common Java Interview Topics 171

2. Mock Interview Questions 173

3. Problem-Solving Strategies 175

4. Hands-On Challenge: Solve a Coding Problem in Java 177

5. Conclusion 180

Chapter 15: Real-World Java Projects 182

Introduction 182

1. Building a Personal Finance Tracker 183

2. Web Application with Spring Boot 189

3. Deploying Your Java Applications 191

4. Building a Full-Stack Java Application 192

5. Conclusion 194

How to Scan a Barcode to Get a Repository

1. **Install a QR/Barcode Scanner** – Ensure you have a barcode or QR code scanner app installed on your smartphone or use a built-in scanner in **GitHub, GitLab, or Bitbucket.**

2. **Open the Scanner** – Launch the scanner app and grant necessary camera permissions.

3. **Scan the Barcode** – Align the barcode within the scanning frame. The scanner will automatically detect and process it.

4. **Follow the Link** – The scanned result will display a **URL to the repository**. Tap the link to open it in your web browser or Git client.

5. **Clone the Repository** – Use **Git clone** with the provided URL to download the repository to your local machine.

Chapter 1: Introduction to Java

What is Java?

Java is one of the most widely used programming languages in the world. It has a robust, simple, and versatile design that allows it to be used for everything from web development and mobile applications to large-scale enterprise systems. Java's design emphasizes portability, reliability, and maintainability.

Imagine you're building a house—Java is like the blueprint for that house. Whether you're building a simple single-family home (a small web app) or a sprawling mansion (a large enterprise system), Java's blueprint remains flexible enough to support any project. That's why it's so popular across different industries—from healthcare and banking to entertainment and gaming.

The Role of Java in Modern Software Development

Java plays a critical role in modern software development because of its "write once, run anywhere" philosophy. It means that once you write a Java program, it can run on any device with a Java Virtual Machine (JVM), whether it's a Windows PC, Mac, or Linux system. This portability makes Java ideal for developers working across platforms.

Real-World Example:

Think about building a mobile app. If you develop a mobile application in Java for Android, it can run on thousands of different devices without modification. Java is also widely used in backend server systems (e.g., websites, databases), making it a core language in full-stack development.

Key Points:

- Java's platform independence.
- Use in cross-platform development (web, mobile, enterprise).
- High performance and scalability.

Why Java is Still One of the Top Programming Languages

Despite the rise of new languages like Python and Go, Java continues to be one of the most widely used programming languages. Why? Several reasons:

1. **Maturity and Stability**: Java has been around for over 25 years, and its maturity means it's well-tested, highly reliable, and backed by a large, active community.

2. **Versatility**: Java can be used for nearly everything—web applications, Android apps, desktop software, backend systems, big data analytics, and more.

3. **Large Ecosystem**: Java has a vast ecosystem of libraries, frameworks, and tools, making development easier and faster. Some popular Java frameworks include Spring, Hibernate, and JavaFX.

4. **Community and Support**: The massive Java community means there's always someone to help. The language is supported by large corporations like Oracle and Google, and it's a top choice for large-scale, enterprise-level applications.

Real-World Example:

Java is the backbone of Android, the world's most popular mobile operating system. In fact, around 70% of Android apps are written in Java.

History and Evolution of Java

Java was created in 1995 by James Gosling and his team at Sun Microsystems (which was later acquired by Oracle). Initially, it was designed to be a language for consumer electronics, but it quickly became clear that Java's design principles (simplicity, portability, and performance) were perfect for internet-based applications.

Java has gone through several iterations:

- **Java 1.0** (1996): The first public version.

- **Java 2** (1998): Introduced key concepts like the Swing GUI toolkit and the Collections framework.

- **Java 5** (2004): Added major features like generics, metadata annotations, and enhanced for-each loops.

- **Java 8** (2014): Introduced lambdas, streams, and the new Date/Time API—modern features that helped Java remain relevant in the age of functional programming.

Setting Up the Development Environment

Before you can start writing Java programs, you need to set up your development environment. This includes installing the Java Development Kit (JDK) and choosing an Integrated Development Environment (IDE) for coding.

Installing Java Development Kit (JDK)

The JDK contains all the tools you need to develop Java applications, including the Java compiler and the Java Runtime Environment (JRE).

Steps to install JDK:

1. **Download JDK:** Go to the official Oracle JDK website and download the latest version of the JDK for your operating system.

2. **Install JDK**: Follow the instructions provided on the website to install Java. Make sure to set the JAVA_HOME environment variable.

3. **Verify Installation**: Open your terminal or command prompt and type:

4. java -version

This will show you the installed version of Java.

Choosing an IDE

An Integrated Development Environment (IDE) helps streamline the coding process by providing features like code completion, debugging tools, and project management.

Popular Java IDEs:

- **IntelliJ IDEA**: A powerful, modern IDE with excellent code analysis and refactoring features. Great for both beginners and professionals.

- **Eclipse**: Another widely used IDE, especially for large Java projects. It's highly customizable and supports numerous plugins.

- **NetBeans**: A solid choice, especially for students and beginners.

You can choose whichever IDE you prefer, but for the sake of this book, we'll assume you're using **IntelliJ IDEA**.

Steps to install IntelliJ IDEA:

1. **Download IntelliJ IDEA**: Visit the IntelliJ IDEA website and download the free Community version.

2. **Install IntelliJ IDEA**: Follow the instructions to install the IDE.

3. **Create Your First Project**: Once installed, open IntelliJ IDEA, create a new Java project, and start coding!

Writing and Running Your First "Hello, World!" Program

Now that you've set up your environment, it's time to write your first Java program!

The Code:

```
public class HelloWorld {

    public static void main(String[] args) {

        System.out.println("Hello, World!");

    }

}
```

Explanation:

1. public class HelloWorld: Defines a class named HelloWorld. In Java, everything is wrapped in a class.

2. public static void main(String[] args): This is the entry point of any Java program. The main method is where the program starts running.

3. System.out.println("Hello, World!");: This line prints "Hello, World!" to the console.

How to Run It:

1. Open IntelliJ IDEA and create a new Java project.

2. Create a new Java class named HelloWorld.

3. Copy and paste the code above into the class.

4. Click the **Run** button (green arrow), and you should see the output in the console:

5. Hello, World!

Key Java Concepts Overview

Now that we've written and executed your first program, let's take a look at some key Java concepts that will help you understand how the language works.

Basic Syntax, Variables, and Operators

Java syntax is the set of rules that defines how Java programs are written. The basic syntax includes:

- **Variables**: A variable is a container that holds data. You must declare a variable with a specific type (e.g., int, double, String).

int age = 30;

double price = 19.99;

String name = "John";

- **Operators**: Operators are symbols that perform operations on variables and values. Common operators include:

  o Arithmetic: +, -, *, /, %

  o Relational: ==, !=, >, <, >=, <=

  o Logical: &&, ||, !

Understanding the Java Compiler and JVM (Java Virtual Machine)

When you write Java code, it doesn't run directly on your computer. Instead, the code needs to be compiled into bytecode, which is then executed by the **JVM**.

- **Java Compiler**: The compiler converts your .java file into a .class file (bytecode).

- **JVM**: The JVM is a program that reads and executes the bytecode, making Java programs platform-independent.

Hands-On Project: Create a "Hello, World!" Java Program

In this section, we'll dive deeper into our first Java project and give you some practical exercises to solidify your understanding.

Step-by-Step Instructions:

1. Open your IDE and create a new Java project.

2. Inside your project, create a new class file named HelloWorld.java.

3. Copy the following code into your HelloWorld.java file:

```java
public class HelloWorld {
    public static void main(String[] args) {
        // Print a greeting message to the console
        System.out.println("Hello, World!");
    }
}
```

4. Run the program. You should see the message **Hello, World!** printed in the console.

Modifying Your Program:

Now that you've created the basic "Hello, World!" program, let's modify it a bit.

1. Change the message from "Hello, World!" to your own name.

2. Add a second System.out.println() statement that prints your age.

3. Run the program again, and see if it displays both lines correctly.

Conclusion

In this chapter, you've learned the basics of Java, including what it is, its role in modern software development, and how to set up your development environment. You've written and run your first Java program and explored key Java concepts like syntax, variables, and the Java Virtual Machine (JVM). Most importantly, you've gained hands-on experience by modifying and running your own Java program.

The next chapter will dive deeper into Java's object-oriented features, where you'll start building more complex programs and learn essential concepts like classes, objects, and methods.

Chapter 2: Understanding the Java Syntax

Java syntax is the foundation for writing Java programs. It defines the rules that make Java code understandable for both humans and machines. By mastering the basic syntax, you'll be able to write clean, functional, and efficient Java programs. In this chapter, we'll break down key Java syntax elements—variables, data types, operators, and control flow statements—and guide you through practical exercises to cement your understanding.

What You'll Need:

Before diving into the code, let's make sure you're all set up to follow along:

1. **Software:**

   o **Java Development Kit (JDK):** To compile and run Java programs. You can download it from Oracle's official site.

   o **IDE (Integrated Development Environment):** We recommend using **IntelliJ IDEA** or **Eclipse**. These IDEs help you write, debug, and run Java programs efficiently.

2. **Hardware:**

   o A computer with at least **2GB of RAM** (recommended) and enough storage space for Java and your IDE.

3. **Prerequisites:**

   o Familiarity with basic programming concepts (e.g., variables, logic) can help, but it's not required for this chapter.

1. Variables, Data Types, and Constants

In Java, variables store data, and each variable has a **data type** that defines the kind of data it can hold. Let's break down Java's data types and see how they work in practice.

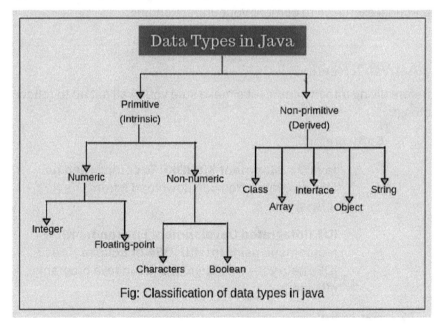

Fig: Classification of data types in java

1.1 Primitive Data Types

Primitive data types represent basic values and serve as the building blocks of more complex data structures. Java has 8 primitive data types:

int (Integer): Used to store whole numbers.

int age = 25;

double (Floating-Point Number): Used for decimal values.

double price = 19.99;

char (Character): Used to store a single character.

char grade = 'A';

boolean (True/False): Used to store true or false values.

boolean isActive = true;

byte: 8-bit integer type, used for small numbers.

byte smallNumber = 100;

short: 16-bit integer type, used for moderately small numbers.

short distance = 1000;

long: 64-bit integer type, used for larger numbers.

long population = 7000000000L; // Notice the 'L' at the end to indicate a long type

float: 32-bit floating-point number for decimal values.

float weight = 55.5f; // Notice the 'f' at the end to indicate a float type

---

1.2 Reference Data Types

Unlike primitive types, reference types refer to objects in memory. They store references (or addresses) to data, not the data itself.

- **String**: A special type for handling text (technically a reference type).

- String name = "John Doe";
- **Arrays**: An ordered collection of values of the same type.
- int[] numbers = {1, 2, 3, 4};

1.3 Constants

In Java, constants are values that do not change once assigned. They are declared using the final keyword.

final double PI = 3.14159; // Constant value of Pi

Constants are typically written in **uppercase letters** with underscores separating words, as per Java conventions.

1.4 Type Conversions

In Java, sometimes you need to convert one data type to another, a process known as **type casting**.

1. **Implicit Conversion** (Widening): Java automatically converts smaller data types to larger ones.

int a = 10;

double b = a; // Implicit conversion from int to double

Explicit Conversion *(Narrowing): You can manually convert larger types to smaller ones.*

double a = 5.75;

int b = (int) a; // Explicit conversion from double to int

---

2. Operators and Expressions

Operators are symbols used to perform operations on variables or values. Java has a variety of operators to manipulate data.

2.1 Arithmetic Operators

These operators are used to perform basic math operations.

- **+**: Addition
- **-**: Subtraction
- *****: Multiplication
- **/**: Division
- **%**: Modulus (remainder)

```
int sum = 10 + 5; // 15
int difference = 10 - 5; // 5
int product = 10 * 5; // 50
int quotient = 10 / 5; // 2
int remainder = 10 % 3; // 1
```

2.2 Relational Operators

These operators compare two values and return a boolean result (true or false).

- **==**: Equal to
- **!=**: Not equal to
- **>**: Greater than
- **<**: Less than
- **>=**: Greater than or equal to
- **<=**: Less than or equal to

```
int x = 10;
int y = 20;
```

boolean result = x < y; // true

2.3 Logical Operators

Logical operators are used to combine multiple conditions.

- **&&**: AND
- **||**: OR
- **!**: NOT

boolean isAdult = true;

boolean hasPermission = false;

boolean canEnter = isAdult && hasPermission; // false (since hasPermission is false)

2.4 Operator Precedence and Shortcuts

Operator precedence determines the order in which operations are performed in an expression. Operators with higher precedence are evaluated first.

Example:

int result = 10 + 2 * 3; // result is 16, not 36, because multiplication has higher precedence than addition

Shortcut operators (also known as compound assignment operators) simplify expressions by combining an operator with an assignment.

int x = 5;

x += 3; // Equivalent to x = x + 3, so x is now 8

---

3. Control Flow Statements

Control flow statements determine the order in which the program's code is executed.

3.1 Conditional Statements: if, else, and switch

if: *Used to execute a block of code if a condition is true.*

```
if (x > 0) {
    System.out.println("x is positive");
}
```

else: *Used to execute a block of code when the condition is false.*

```
if (x > 0) {
    System.out.println("x is positive");
} else {
    System.out.println("x is not positive");
}
```

switch: *Used to select one of many blocks of code to execute based on the value of a variable.*

```
switch (day) {
    case 1: System.out.println("Monday"); break;
    case 2: System.out.println("Tuesday"); break;
    default: System.out.println("Invalid day");
}
```

3.2 Loops: while, for, and do-while

Loops are used to repeatedly execute a block of code.

while loop: *Repeats as long as a condition is true.*

```
int i = 0;
while (i < 5) {
    System.out.println(i);
    i++;
}
```

for loop: *Useful when the number of iterations is known.*

```
for (int i = 0; i < 5; i++) {
    System.out.println(i);
}
```

do-while loop: *Always executes the block of code at least once, even if the condition is false.*

```
int i = 0;
do {
    System.out.println(i);
    i++;
} while (i < 5);
```

3.3 Control Flow Keywords: break, continue, and return

break: *Exits from a loop or switch statement.*

```
for (int i = 0; i < 10; i++) {
    if (i == 5) {
        break;  // Exits the loop when i equals 5
    }
    System.out.println(i);
}
```

continue: *Skips the current iteration and moves to the next one.*

```
for (int i = 0; i < 10; i++) {
    if (i == 5) {
        continue; // Skips printing when i equals 5
    }
    System.out.println(i);
}
```

return: Exits a method and optionally returns a value.

```
public int sum(int a, int b) {
    return a + b; // Returns the sum of a and b
}
```

---

4. Hands-On Project: Build a Simple Calculator

Now that you've learned the basic syntax, let's implement a **simple calculator** that performs basic arithmetic operations (addition, subtraction, multiplication, division).

Step-by-Step Instructions:

Create a New Java Class: Create a new Java file named Calculator.java.

Define the Calculator Class:

```
public class Calculator {
    public static void main(String[] args) {
        // Declare variables
        double num1 = 10.5;
        double num2 = 5.5;
        double result;
```

```
// Addition
result = num1 + num2;
System.out.println("Addition: " + result);

// Subtraction
result = num1 - num2;
System.out.println("Subtraction: " + result);

// Multiplication
result = num1 * num2;
System.out.println("Multiplication: " + result);

// Division
result = num1 / num2;
System.out.println("Division: " + result);
  }
}
```

1. **Run the Program**: Run the program, and you should see the results of the basic arithmetic operations printed on the console.

Conclusion

In this chapter, you've learned the essential building blocks of Java syntax—variables, data types, operators, and control flow statements. You've also gained practical experience by building a simple calculator. By understanding these fundamental concepts, you're now ready to dive deeper into Java programming and explore more complex topics like object-oriented programming, classes, and methods.

Next Steps:

- Experiment with the calculator by adding more operations (e.g., modulus, square root).

- Try adding user input functionality to make the calculator interactive.

Chapter 3: Mastering Object-Oriented Programming (OOP) in Java

Welcome to Chapter 3, where we begin diving into the heart of Java programming: **Object-Oriented Programming (OOP)**. If you've already worked with basic syntax and control flow, you're now ready to move on to a more powerful way to structure and manage your code. In this chapter, you will learn the four fundamental principles of OOP in Java: **Encapsulation, Inheritance, Polymorphism, and Abstraction**. These principles are not just theory—they are the foundation for writing efficient, maintainable, and scalable code.

By the end of this chapter, you will have built your own **Car class** and implemented **encapsulation**, one of the core tenets of OOP. You'll also understand how to create and manage objects, and how to use the principles of OOP to make your Java programs more organized and easier to maintain.

What You'll Need:

Before you start, let's make sure you have everything set up to follow along with this chapter:

- **Software:**
  - **Java Development Kit (JDK):** You should already have this installed from Chapter 1. If not, please download and install it from the Oracle JDK website.

- o **IDE (Integrated Development Environment):** We recommend **IntelliJ IDEA** or **Eclipse** for coding. These IDEs provide helpful tools like code completion, debugging, and project management to make Java programming easier.

- **Hardware:**
  - o A computer with at least **2GB of RAM** and some free storage space for the JDK and your projects.

- **Prerequisites:**
  - o You should be comfortable with the basics of Java syntax, variables, and basic control flow, which were covered in the previous chapter.

1. The Basics of Object-Oriented Programming (OOP) in Java

What is OOP?

Object-Oriented Programming (OOP) is a programming paradigm that organizes software design around **objects**, rather than functions or logic. In OOP, an object is a self-contained unit that contains both data and methods that operate on that data.

To put it simply, think of OOP as a way to model the world by using real-world entities. For example, in a car manufacturing application, you can think of a **Car** as an object, which has properties (data) such as **speed** and **fuel**, and methods (functions) such as **accelerate** and **brake**.

The Four Key Principles of OOP:

Encapsulation

- ○ **What is Encapsulation?**
  - ▪ Encapsulation is the technique of bundling data (variables) and methods that work on the data within one unit (or class). It's like putting things in a box: the internal workings (data and methods) are hidden from the outside, and you can only interact with the data through specified methods.
  - ▪ In Java, encapsulation is achieved through **private** fields and **public** methods, which are known as **getters** and **setters**.

2. **Inheritance**

- ○ **What is Inheritance?**
  - ▪ Inheritance is a mechanism where one class acquires the properties and behaviors (fields and methods) of another class. It allows for code reusability and makes it easier to maintain and extend your programs.
  - ▪ In Java, inheritance is achieved by using the extends keyword.

3. **Polymorphism**

- ○ **What is Polymorphism?**
  - ▪ Polymorphism allows objects of different classes to be treated as objects of a common superclass. It lets you define one interface but have different implementations. Polymorphism helps you write more flexible and reusable code.

- There are two types of polymorphism in Java:

    - **Compile-time polymorphism (Method Overloading)**

    - **Runtime polymorphism (Method Overriding)**

4. **Abstraction**

    o **What is Abstraction?**

        - Abstraction is the process of hiding the implementation details and showing only the essential features of an object. In Java, you can achieve abstraction using **abstract classes** and **interfaces**. This helps in simplifying complex systems by focusing on high-level interactions.

2. The Difference Between Classes and Objects

At the heart of OOP are **classes** and **objects**. While they are closely related, they serve different purposes:

- **Class**: A class is a blueprint or template for creating objects. It defines the attributes (variables) and behaviors (methods) that the objects of the class will have. A class is like a recipe for making cookies.

- **Object**: An object is an instance of a class. It is the actual thing that exists in memory when the class is instantiated. Continuing with the cookie analogy, the cookie is the object, and the recipe is the class.

Example:

```
// This is a class called Car
```

```java
public class Car {
    String color;
    int speed;

    public void accelerate() {
        speed += 10;
        System.out.println("The car is accelerating.");
    }
}


// This is how you create objects (instances) of the Car class
public class Main {
    public static void main(String[] args) {
        // Creating objects of the Car class
        Car myCar = new Car();
        myCar.color = "Red";
        myCar.speed = 0;

        // Calling methods on the object
        myCar.accelerate();
    }
}
```

Here, the Car class defines the properties (color and speed) and the behavior (accelerate method). The myCar object is an instance of the Car class.

3. Encapsulation

Encapsulation is one of the fundamental concepts in OOP. It involves **hiding** the internal state of an object and requiring all interaction with that state to be done through public methods. This makes the system more secure and easier to maintain.

Why Use Encapsulation?

- **Control Access**: You can control how the data in your object is modified, ensuring that no invalid changes are made to the internal state.

- **Maintainability**: If you need to change how data is handled inside your object, you can do so without affecting the code that interacts with the object.

Implementing Encapsulation in Java

1. **Private Fields**: Fields (variables) are made private so that they cannot be accessed directly from outside the class.

2. **Public Methods**: Methods (getters and setters) are provided to allow controlled access to the fields.

Hands-On Example: Build a Car Class with Encapsulation

Let's build a **Car** class that uses **encapsulation** to manage its properties.

Create the Car Class:

```
public class Car {
    // Private fields (attributes)
    private String color;
    private int speed;
```

```java
// Getter for color
public String getColor() {
    return color;
}


// Setter for color
public void setColor(String color) {
    this.color = color;
}


// Getter for speed
public int getSpeed() {
    return speed;
}


// Setter for speed
public void setSpeed(int speed) {
    if (speed >= 0) {
        this.speed = speed;
    } else {
        System.out.println("Speed cannot be negative.");
    }
}


// Method to accelerate
```

```
public void accelerate() {
    speed += 10;
    System.out.println("The car is accelerating. Current speed: " +
speed);
}


// Method to brake
public void brake() {
    if (speed > 0) {
        speed -= 10;
        System.out.println("The car is braking. Current speed: " +
speed);
    } else {
        System.out.println("The car is already stopped.");
    }
}
}
```

Create the Main Class:

```
public class Main {
    public static void main(String[] args) {
        // Create a new Car object
        Car myCar = new Car();


        // Set the car's color and speed using setters
        myCar.setColor("Red");
        myCar.setSpeed(0);
```

```
// Print car details
System.out.println("Car color: " + myCar.getColor());
System.out.println("Initial speed: " + myCar.getSpeed());

// Accelerate and brake the car
myCar.accelerate();
myCar.accelerate();
myCar.brake();
myCar.brake();
    }
}
```

Explanation:

- **Private Fields**: The color and speed attributes are marked as private. This means they cannot be accessed directly outside of the Car class.

- **Public Methods**: We provide getColor(), setColor(), getSpeed(), and setSpeed() methods to allow controlled access to these private fields.

- **Logic in Setters**: In the setter for speed, we added a check to ensure the speed cannot be set to a negative number.

Testing Your Code:

1. Compile and run your program.

2. Observe how the car's speed and color are managed via getters and setters.

3. Try to set the car's speed to a negative number and see how the program prevents it.

---

4. Real-World Applications of Encapsulation

Encapsulation is widely used in many real-world scenarios, from managing user accounts to controlling access to sensitive data. Here's how encapsulation can be applied to a **banking application**:

- **Account Class:** In a banking system, the account balance would be a private field, and methods like deposit() and withdraw() would allow controlled changes to the balance.

```
public class Account {

    private double balance;

    public double getBalance() {
        return balance;
    }

    public void deposit(double amount) {
        if (amount > 0) {
            balance += amount;
            System.out.println("Deposited: " + amount);
        } else {
            System.out.println("Amount must be positive.");
        }
    }
}
```

```
public void withdraw(double amount) {
    if (amount > 0 && amount <= balance) {
        balance -= amount;
        System.out.println("Withdrew: " + amount);
    } else {
        System.out.println("Invalid withdrawal amount.");
    }
}
}
```

Conclusion

In this chapter, you learned the foundational concept of **Object-Oriented Programming (OOP)**, with a focus on **encapsulation**. We explored the basics of classes and objects, and how encapsulation allows you to control access to the internal state of an object, making your code more secure and maintainable.

By building a **Car class** and implementing encapsulation, you gained hands-on experience with one of the most powerful features of Java. As you progress through the next chapters, you'll expand on these concepts by learning about **inheritance**, **polymorphism**, and **abstraction**, which will allow you to write more complex and reusable code.

Next Steps:

- Try adding more functionality to your Car class, such as a method to check if the car has enough fuel to accelerate.

- Experiment with creating different objects (e.g., Truck, Motorcycle) and see how you can use **inheritance** to build common functionality across these objects.

Let's continue to master OOP in Java!

Chapter 4: Inheritance and Polymorphism

In this chapter, we'll dive deep into two of the most important and powerful concepts in Object-Oriented Programming (OOP): **Inheritance** and **Polymorphism**. These concepts allow developers to create more flexible, reusable, and maintainable code, which is essential for writing scalable applications.

By the end of this chapter, you will understand how inheritance enables code reuse and promotes scalability, and how polymorphism—both **method overloading** and **method overriding**—lets you write adaptable and efficient programs. We'll also provide hands-on examples and real-world applications that help you practice these concepts.

What You'll Need:

Before we begin, let's make sure you're all set up:

1. **Software:**

   o **Java Development Kit (JDK):** This is essential for compiling and running Java programs. If you haven't done so already, download and install it from Oracle's official site.

   o **IDE (Integrated Development Environment):** We recommend **IntelliJ IDEA** or **Eclipse** for writing Java code. These tools provide helpful features such as syntax highlighting, auto-completion, and debugging support.

   o

2. **Hardware**:

   o   A computer with at least **2GB of RAM** and some free space to store your code and projects.

3. **Prerequisites**:

   o   A basic understanding of Java syntax, classes, and methods (from previous chapters). You should also be familiar with concepts like variables, loops, and conditionals.

1. What is Inheritance?

Inheritance is one of the cornerstones of **Object-Oriented Programming (OOP)**. It allows a class to inherit properties and behaviors (fields and methods) from another class, promoting code reuse and helping to establish a natural hierarchy between classes. Inheritance forms a relationship between the parent class (also known as the **superclass**) and the child class (also called the **subclass**).

How Inheritance Enables Code Reuse and Promotes Scalability:

1. **Code Reuse**: Inheritance allows subclasses to reuse code from the parent class, which minimizes redundancy and makes the program more efficient.

   o   For example, if we have a class called Animal that has a makeSound() method, we don't need to write this method in every animal class like Dog or Cat. Instead, Dog and Cat can inherit this method from Animal.

2. **Scalability**: As your program grows, inheritance allows you to create specialized classes without repeating code. If you need to add a new behavior or attribute to a family of

classes, you can simply modify the parent class, and all subclasses automatically inherit that change.

- o Imagine adding a new fly() method to a Bird class. All subclasses of Bird (like Sparrow or Eagle) will inherit this method without any additional effort.

The super Keyword and the Role of Constructors in Inheritance:

The super keyword is used in Java to refer to the immediate parent class. It is commonly used in two main ways:

1. **Calling Parent Class Constructors**: When creating a subclass, you may need to initialize the parent class before initializing the subclass itself. The super() keyword is used to call the parent class's constructor.

2. **Accessing Parent Class Methods and Fields**: You can use super.methodName() to call a method from the parent class if you've overridden it in the subclass.

Example: Implementing Inheritance in Java

Let's look at an example where we create an Animal superclass, and then define a Dog subclass that inherits from Animal.

```
// Parent class (superclass)
public class Animal {
    // Field
    String name;

    // Constructor
    public Animal(String name) {
```

```java
        this.name = name;
    }


    // Method
    public void makeSound() {
        System.out.println("Animal makes a sound");
    }
}


// Child class (subclass)
public class Dog extends Animal {


    // Constructor
    public Dog(String name) {
        // Calling the parent class constructor
        super(name);
    }


    // Overriding the parent class method
    @Override
    public void makeSound() {
        System.out.println(name + " says Woof!");
    }
}
```

In this example:

- The Dog class inherits the makeSound() method and the name field from the Animal class.

- We use super(name) to call the constructor of the Animal class and initialize the name field.

2. Polymorphism: Method Overloading and Overriding

Polymorphism is another powerful feature of OOP that allows an object to take many forms. There are two types of polymorphism in Java: **method overloading** (compile-time polymorphism) and **method overriding** (runtime polymorphism). These concepts enable you to write flexible, maintainable code that can adapt to different situations.

2.1 Method Overloading (Compile-Time Polymorphism)

Method overloading occurs when two or more methods in the same class have the same name but different parameters (either in number, type, or both). The Java compiler determines which method to call at **compile time** based on the method signature.

Example: Overloading the add() Method

```
public class Calculator {

    // Method to add two integers
    public int add(int a, int b) {
        return a + b;
    }
```

```
// Overloaded method to add three integers
public int add(int a, int b, int c) {
    return a + b + c;
}

// Overloaded method to add two doubles
public double add(double a, double b) {
    return a + b;
}
}
```

In this example:

- We have three add() methods, each with a different signature.
- The appropriate method is chosen based on the number and type of arguments passed when the method is called.

2.2 Method Overriding (Runtime Polymorphism)

Method overriding occurs when a subclass provides a specific implementation for a method that is already defined in its superclass. The version of the method that gets executed is determined **at runtime** based on the object type (whether it's a parent class or subclass object).

Example: Overriding the makeSound() Method

```
public class Animal {
    public void makeSound() {
        System.out.println("Animal makes a sound");
    }
}
```

```
}

public class Dog extends Animal {
    @Override
    public void makeSound() {
        System.out.println("Dog says Woof!");
    }
}

public class Main {
    public static void main(String[] args) {
        Animal myAnimal = new Animal();
        Animal myDog = new Dog();  // Upcasting

        myAnimal.makeSound(); // Animal makes a sound
        myDog.makeSound();    // Dog says Woof!
    }
}
```

In this example:

- Both Animal and Dog classes have a makeSound() method.
- At runtime, Java chooses the correct version of the method to call based on the object type (myAnimal or myDog), even though both variables are of type Animal.

3. Hands-On Project: Extend the Car Class with Subclasses

Now, let's put inheritance and polymorphism into practice. We will extend the Car class by creating two subclasses: ElectricCar and SportsCar. We'll implement **inheritance** and **polymorphism** to extend functionality and override methods.

Step 1: Define the Car Class (Superclass)

```
public class Car {
    private String model;
    private int speed;

    public Car(String model) {
        this.model = model;
        this.speed = 0;
    }

    public void accelerate() {
        speed += 10;
        System.out.println(model + " is accelerating. Speed: " + speed);
    }

    public void brake() {
        if (speed > 0) {
            speed -= 10;
            System.out.println(model + " is braking. Speed: " + speed);
```

```
    } else {
        System.out.println(model + " is already stopped.");
    }
}


public String getModel() {
    return model;
}
}
```

Step 2: Create the ElectricCar Class (Subclass)

```
public class ElectricCar extends Car {

    public ElectricCar(String model) {
        super(model);
    }

    // Overriding accelerate method
    @Override
    public void accelerate() {
        super.accelerate(); // Calling the parent class method
        System.out.println(getModel() + " is accelerating silently.");
    }

    // Adding a new feature unique to ElectricCar
```

```java
public void chargeBattery() {
    System.out.println(getModel() + " is charging the battery.");
}
}
```

Step 3: Create the SportsCar Class (Subclass)

```java
public class SportsCar extends Car {

    public SportsCar(String model) {
        super(model);
    }

    // Overriding accelerate method
    @Override
    public void accelerate() {
        super.accelerate();
        System.out.println(getModel() + " is accelerating rapidly! Vroom Vroom!");
    }

    // Adding a new feature unique to SportsCar
    public void turboBoost() {
        System.out.println(getModel() + " is activating turbo boost!");
    }
}
```

Step 4: Test Your Classes in the Main Class

```
public class Main {
    public static void main(String[] args) {
        Car myCar = new Car("Generic Car");
        Car myElectricCar = new ElectricCar("Tesla Model 3");
        Car mySportsCar = new SportsCar("Ferrari 488");

        myCar.accelerate();
        myElectricCar.accelerate();
        mySportsCar.accelerate();

        // Additional functionality specific to subclasses
        ElectricCar tesla = (ElectricCar) myElectricCar;
        tesla.chargeBattery();

        SportsCar ferrari = (SportsCar) mySportsCar;
        ferrari.turboBoost();
    }
}
```

4. Real-World Application: Using Polymorphism in a Payment System

Now let's apply polymorphism in a **real-world application**: a **payment system**. The goal is to create different types of payment methods (e.g., CreditCard, PayPal, and BankTransfer) and override the processPayment() method in each class.

Step 1: Define a Payment Interface

```java
public interface PaymentMethod {
    void processPayment(double amount);
}
```

Step 2: Implement Different Payment Methods

```java
public class CreditCard implements PaymentMethod {
    @Override
    public void processPayment(double amount) {
        System.out.println("Processing credit card payment of $" +
amount);
    }
}


public class PayPal implements PaymentMethod {
    @Override
    public void processPayment(double amount) {
        System.out.println("Processing PayPal payment of $" +
amount);
    }
}


public class BankTransfer implements PaymentMethod {
    @Override
    public void processPayment(double amount) {
```

```
    System.out.println("Processing bank transfer payment of $" +
amount);
  }
}
```

Step 3: Test the Payment System

```
public class PaymentSystem {
  public static void main(String[] args) {
    PaymentMethod creditCard = new CreditCard();
    PaymentMethod payPal = new PayPal();
    PaymentMethod bankTransfer = new BankTransfer();

    creditCard.processPayment(100.00);
    payPal.processPayment(250.50);
    bankTransfer.processPayment(500.75);
  }
}
```

Conclusion

In this chapter, you learned about **inheritance** and **polymorphism**—two of the most powerful concepts in Java. You saw how **inheritance** allows code reuse and scalability, and how **polymorphism** (both method overloading and method overriding) helps you build flexible, maintainable code. By working through hands-on examples, including extending the Car class and implementing polymorphism in a payment system, you gained practical experience in applying these principles to real-world applications.

Chapter 5: Abstraction and Interfaces

In the previous chapters, we've delved into the foundational principles of Object-Oriented Programming (OOP), such as **encapsulation, inheritance**, and **polymorphism**. In this chapter, we'll explore two crucial OOP concepts that further empower your ability to design flexible and scalable software systems: **Abstraction** and **Interfaces**.

Abstraction is the process of hiding the implementation details and exposing only the necessary functionality. It helps to simplify complex systems by focusing on high-level interactions. Interfaces, on the other hand, provide a way to define common behavior across unrelated classes without forcing them into a rigid inheritance structure.

Interfaces vs. Abstract Classes

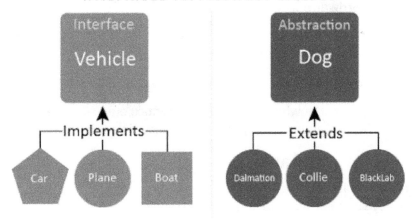

You'll learn about **abstract classes** and **interfaces**, the differences between them, and when to use each in your Java programs. We'll also implement a **Payment Interface** for handling various types of payments (credit card, PayPal, etc.) to demonstrate these concepts in action.

By the end of this chapter, you'll have a deeper understanding of abstraction and interfaces, and you'll be equipped to apply these concepts in your own projects.

What You'll Need:

Before diving into the code, ensure that you have the following set up:

1. **Software:**

   o **Java Development Kit (JDK):** You should already have this installed from previous chapters. If not, please download and install it from the Oracle JDK website.

   o **IDE (Integrated Development Environment):** IntelliJ IDEA or Eclipse is recommended for a better coding experience. They offer helpful features like auto-completion, debugging, and syntax highlighting.

2. **Hardware:**

   o A computer with at least **2GB of RAM** and sufficient storage for Java projects.

3. **Prerequisites:**

   o Knowledge of basic Java syntax, classes, inheritance, and polymorphism, as covered in earlier chapters.

1. Abstract Classes vs. Interfaces

Before we dive into the hands-on project, let's start by discussing the two key abstractions in Java: **abstract classes** and **interfaces**. These are both used to define methods that a class must implement, but they are different in terms of how they are used and when to choose one over the other.

1.1 Abstract Classes

An **abstract class** is a class that cannot be instantiated (i.e., you cannot create an object of an abstract class directly). It is meant to be inherited by other classes, and it can contain both **abstract methods** (which have no body and must be implemented by subclasses) and **concrete methods** (which are fully implemented in the abstract class itself).

When to Use an Abstract Class:

- When you want to provide some shared functionality to all subclasses but also want to allow subclasses to implement their own versions of certain methods.

- When your class shares a common **base functionality** but needs to have its own unique implementation.

Key Features:

1. **Abstract Methods**: Methods that are declared but not defined in the abstract class. Subclasses must provide their own implementations.

2. **Concrete Methods**: Fully implemented methods that can be inherited by subclasses.

Example of an Abstract Class:

```
abstract class Payment {
    // Abstract method (no body)
    public abstract void processPayment(double amount);

    // Concrete method (fully implemented)
    public void logTransaction() {
```

```
System.out.println("Logging transaction...");
    }
}
```

In this example:

- processPayment() is an **abstract method**, and each subclass must provide its own implementation of this method.

- logTransaction() is a **concrete method** that provides a default behavior that all subclasses can inherit.

1.2 Interfaces

An **interface** in Java is like a contract that a class must follow. It contains only **abstract methods** (before Java 8) and **constants** (fields declared as static final). Starting from Java 8, interfaces can also contain **default methods** (methods with a body) and **static methods**.

When to Use an Interface:

- When you need to define a contract for a class to follow, but you don't want to dictate the class's inheritance structure.

- When you want to implement **multiple inheritance** (Java doesn't support multiple class inheritance, but classes can implement multiple interfaces).

Key Features:

1. **Abstract Methods**: All methods in an interface are abstract by default (unless they are default or static methods).

2. **Default Methods**: Methods with an implementation provided in the interface itself.

3. **Constants**: Fields are public, static, and final by default.

Example of an Interface:

```java
interface PaymentMethod {
    void processPayment(double amount); // Abstract method

    // Default method
    default void logTransaction() {
        System.out.println("Logging transaction via PaymentMethod interface...");
    }
}
```

In this example:

- processPayment() is an **abstract method.**

- logTransaction() is a **default method** that provides a default implementation.

2. Key Differences Between Abstract Classes and Interfaces

Feature	Abstract Class	Interface
Methods	Can have both abstract and concrete methods	Only abstract methods (before Java 8)
Multiple Inheritance	A class can only extend one abstract class	A class can implement multiple interfaces
Constructors	Can have constructors	Cannot have constructors
Field Types	Can have instance variables (fields)	Can only have static final variables
Usage	Used for classes with shared functionality	Used to define a contract (no implementation)

Summary:

- **Use an abstract class** when you want to provide shared code but also require some customization in subclasses.

- **Use an interface** when you need to define a set of methods that different classes must implement but don't need to share any implementation.

3. Using Interfaces for Flexibility

Interfaces allow for flexibility in your code by enabling you to define common behavior across different classes. Since Java supports **multiple interface inheritance,** you can implement several interfaces, allowing your classes to "inherit" multiple behaviors.

Example of Flexibility with Interfaces:

Let's say we have different types of payment methods (CreditCard, PayPal, BankTransfer), and we want to implement a common interface for all of them.

4. Hands-On Project: Design a Payment Interface

Now, let's create a practical example where we design a **Payment Interface** and implement it for multiple types of payment methods, such as credit card, PayPal, and bank transfer.

Step 1: Define the IPayment Interface

```
interface IPayment {

    void processPayment(double amount); // Abstract method


    // Default method
```

```
default void logTransaction() {

    System.out.println("Logging payment transaction...");

}

}
```

The IPayment interface defines a processPayment() method that each implementing class must provide. The logTransaction() method is a default method that provides a default implementation, which can be overridden if necessary.

Step 2: Implement the Interface for Different Payment Methods

```
class CreditCardPayment implements IPayment {

    @Override

    public void processPayment(double amount) {

        System.out.println("Processing credit card payment of $" +
amount);

    }

}


class PayPalPayment implements IPayment {

    @Override

    public void processPayment(double amount) {

        System.out.println("Processing PayPal payment of $" +
amount);

    }

}
```

```java
class BankTransferPayment implements IPayment {
    @Override
    public void processPayment(double amount) {
        System.out.println("Processing bank transfer payment of $" + amount);
    }
}
```

Each payment method implements the processPayment() method from the IPayment interface.

Step 3: Test the Payment Methods in the Main Class

```java
public class PaymentSystem {
    public static void main(String[] args) {
        IPayment creditCard = new CreditCardPayment();
        IPayment payPal = new PayPalPayment();
        IPayment bankTransfer = new BankTransferPayment();

        creditCard.processPayment(100.00);
        payPal.processPayment(250.50);
        bankTransfer.processPayment(500.75);

        // Log transactions (using default method from interface)
        creditCard.logTransaction();
        payPal.logTransaction();
        bankTransfer.logTransaction();
    }
```

/

Step 4: Explanation of the Code

1. **IPayment Interface:**

   o The IPayment interface defines two methods:

      ▪ processPayment(double amount): This must be implemented by any class that uses the IPayment interface.

      ▪ logTransaction(): A default method that can be used directly or overridden by implementing classes.

2. **Payment Methods:**

   o The classes CreditCardPayment, PayPalPayment, and BankTransferPayment each implement the processPayment() method from the IPayment interface.

3. **Main Class:**

   o In the PaymentSystem class, we create instances of CreditCardPayment, PayPalPayment, and BankTransferPayment. Each object implements the IPayment interface, allowing us to call processPayment() and logTransaction() on them.

5. Real-World Applications of Abstraction and Interfaces

Interfaces and abstraction play a crucial role in real-world applications, particularly when building large, complex systems. Some examples include:

- **Payment Processing Systems**: In e-commerce platforms, payment gateways need to support different types of payment methods, like credit cards, PayPal, and bank transfers. Using interfaces allows these different methods to be implemented in a flexible way.

- **Vehicle Management Systems**: In a vehicle management application, you might have a Vehicle interface, with implementations like Car, Truck, and Motorcycle. Each class implements common behaviors like start(), stop(), and fuelEfficiency().

- **Network Communication Systems**: When building a network system, interfaces can define common methods for handling requests, sending data, and receiving data. Different types of connections (e.g., TCP, UDP) can implement the same interface but with different behaviors.

Conclusion

In this chapter, we explored the concepts of **abstraction** and **interfaces** in Java. You learned the differences between **abstract classes** and **interfaces**, when to use each, and how they contribute to creating flexible, scalable, and maintainable code.

Through the hands-on project, you implemented a **Payment Interface** and explored how polymorphism allows you to define common behavior across different payment methods like credit card, PayPal, and bank transfer. You also gained experience working with **default methods** in interfaces, which add even more flexibility.

Chapter 6: Working with Collections in Java

In the world of Java programming, **collections** are among the most powerful and frequently used data structures. They enable you to store, retrieve, and manipulate data efficiently. Whether you're developing a small application or building a large system, understanding collections is crucial for managing data in an organized and effective manner.

In this chapter, we will dive into the **Java Collections Framework**. We'll explore different types of collections, such as **Lists**, **Sets**, and **Maps**, and learn how to use them to manage your data. We will also cover how to **sort**, **filter**, and **manipulate** data within these collections, providing you with the tools to handle complex data efficiently.

The chapter culminates in a **hands-on project**, where you will build a **Library Management System** that uses **ArrayList**, **HashSet**, and **HashMap** to store and manage books, authors, and book lookups by ID.

What You'll Need:

Before diving into the code, make sure you have the following set up:

1. **Software:**

   o **Java Development Kit (JDK):** If you haven't already installed the JDK, you can download it from Oracle's official website.

   o **IDE (Integrated Development Environment):** We recommend using **IntelliJ IDEA** or **Eclipse** for a smoother coding experience.

2. **Hardware**:

   o A computer with **at least 2GB of RAM** and enough storage to manage your projects.

3. **Prerequisites**:

   o Familiarity with basic Java concepts, such as classes, objects, methods, and control flow (loops and conditionals). If you've followed the previous chapters, you should be well-prepared for this one.

---

1. Introduction to Collections

The **Java Collections Framework** provides a set of classes and interfaces that implement commonly used collections. A collection is simply a group of objects stored in a specific way. The framework is designed to make it easier to manage and process data efficiently in Java.

The Need for Collections:

Before collections, developers had to rely on arrays to store data. However, arrays have significant limitations:

- Fixed size: Once an array is created, its size cannot be changed.

- Limited functionality: You have to write custom logic for sorting, filtering, and manipulating data in arrays.

The **Collections Framework** solves these problems by providing flexible and powerful data structures. These include:

- Dynamic resizing

- Built-in methods for sorting, searching, and manipulating data

---

Understanding the Collection Framework

The **Collection Framework** is divided into two main parts:

1. **Interfaces**: Define the general structure and behavior of collections. Common interfaces include **List**, **Set**, and **Map**.

2. **Implementations**: Provide concrete implementations of these interfaces. For example, **ArrayList**, **HashSet**, and **HashMap** are implementations of the **List**, **Set**, and **Map** interfaces, respectively.

In this chapter, we will focus on three key interfaces:

- **List**

- **Set**

- **Map**

Each of these interfaces has unique characteristics and is suited for different use cases.

---

2. Common Interfaces: List, Set, Map

2.1 List Interface

A **List** is an ordered collection of elements that allows duplicates. Elements in a list can be accessed by their index (position).

Common Implementations of List:

- **ArrayList**: A dynamic array that resizes itself as elements are added or removed. It allows fast access by index but may be slower when inserting or removing elements from the middle of the list.

- **LinkedList**: A doubly linked list that allows for efficient insertion and deletion of elements, but slower access by index compared to ArrayList.

Example: Working with ArrayList

import java.util.ArrayList;

```
public class ListExample {
    public static void main(String[] args) {
        ArrayList<String> books = new ArrayList<>();
        books.add("The Great Gatsby");
        books.add("To Kill a Mockingbird");
        books.add("1984");

        System.out.println("Books: " + books);
        System.out.println("First book: " + books.get(0)); // Access by index
    }
}
```

2.2 Set Interface

A **Set** is a collection that does not allow duplicates. The elements in a set are unordered, meaning the order in which elements are added is not necessarily the order in which they are iterated.

Common Implementations of Set:

- **HashSet**: A set that uses a hash table for storage. It provides constant-time performance for the basic operations (add, remove, contains), but does not guarantee the order of elements.

- **LinkedHashSet**: Similar to HashSet but maintains the insertion order.

Example: Working with HashSet

```java
import java.util.HashSet;

public class SetExample {
    public static void main(String[] args) {
        HashSet<String> authors = new HashSet<>();
        authors.add("J.K. Rowling");
        authors.add("George Orwell");
        authors.add("J.K. Rowling"); // Duplicate, won't be added

        System.out.println("Authors: " + authors);
    }
}
```

2.3 Map Interface

A **Map** is a collection of key-value pairs, where each key maps to exactly one value. Maps do not allow duplicate keys, but multiple values can be associated with the same key.

Common Implementations of Map:

- **HashMap:** A hash table-based implementation that allows fast access to values based on keys. It does not guarantee the order of the entries.

- **LinkedHashMap:** Similar to HashMap but maintains the insertion order of keys.

Example: Working with HashMap

```java
import java.util.HashMap;
```

```java
public class MapExample {
    public static void main(String[] args) {
        HashMap<Integer, String> booksById = new HashMap<>();
        booksById.put(1, "The Great Gatsby");
        booksById.put(2, "1984");
        booksById.put(3, "To Kill a Mockingbird");

        System.out.println("Book with ID 2: " + booksById.get(2)); // Access by key
    }
}
```

---

3. Working with Lists, Sets, and Maps

Now that we've explored the basic interfaces, let's take a deeper look at how we can **sort**, **filter**, and **manipulate** data within **List**, **Set**, and **Map** collections.

3.1 Sorting Data in a List

Java provides a built-in utility class called **Collections** for sorting lists.

Example: Sorting an ArrayList

```java
import java.util.ArrayList;
import java.util.Collections;

public class SortListExample {
    public static void main(String[] args) {
        ArrayList<String> books = new ArrayList<>();
```

```
books.add("The Great Gatsby");
books.add("1984");
books.add("To Kill a Mockingbird");

Collections.sort(books); // Sorting the list in ascending order

System.out.println("Sorted Books: " + books);
    }
}
```

3.2 Filtering Data in a List

You can use the **Stream API** (available in Java 8 and later) to filter data in a collection. This allows you to apply filters, such as returning only items that match a certain condition.

Example: Filtering a List of Books

```
import java.util.ArrayList;
import java.util.List;
import java.util.stream.Collectors;

public class FilterListExample {
    public static void main(String[] args) {
        ArrayList<String> books = new ArrayList<>();
        books.add("The Great Gatsby");
        books.add("1984");
        books.add("To Kill a Mockingbird");

        // Filter books that contain the word '1984'
```

```
List<String> filteredBooks = books.stream()
    .filter(book -> book.contains("1984"))
    .collect(Collectors.toList());


System.out.println("Filtered Books: " + filteredBooks);
    }
}
```

3.3 Manipulating Data in a Set

Unlike lists, **sets** don't allow duplicates. However, you can manipulate data in a set by adding and removing elements.

Example: Adding and Removing Elements from a Set

```
import java.util.HashSet;


public class ManipulateSetExample {
    public static void main(String[] args) {
        HashSet<String> authors = new HashSet<>();
        authors.add("J.K. Rowling");
        authors.add("George Orwell");


        // Trying to add a duplicate
        authors.add("J.K. Rowling"); // Duplicate, won't be added


        // Removing an author
        authors.remove("George Orwell");


        System.out.println("Authors: " + authors);
```

```
}
}
```

3.4 Manipulating Data in a Map

You can manipulate data in a map by adding, removing, or updating key-value pairs.

Example: Adding, Updating, and Removing Entries in a Map

```java
import java.util.HashMap;

public class ManipulateMapExample {
    public static void main(String[] args) {
        HashMap<Integer, String> booksById = new HashMap<>();
        booksById.put(1, "The Great Gatsby");
        booksById.put(2, "1984");

        // Adding a new book
        booksById.put(3, "To Kill a Mockingbird");

        // Updating an existing book
        booksById.put(2, "Brave New World");

        // Removing a book
        booksById.remove(1);

        System.out.println("Books by ID: " + booksById);
    }
}
```

4. Hands-On Project: Build a Library Management System

Now that you've learned how to work with collections in Java, let's apply that knowledge in a practical project: a **Library Management System**.

Step 1: Define the Book Class

```java
public class Book {
    private int id;
    private String title;
    private String author;

    public Book(int id, String title, String author) {
        this.id = id;
        this.title = title;
        this.author = author;
    }

    public int getId() {
        return id;
    }

    public String getTitle() {
        return title;
    }
}
```

```java
public String getAuthor() {
    return author;
}


@Override
public String toString() {
    return "Book{ID=" + id + ", Title='" + title + "', Author='" +
author + "'}";
    }
}
```

Step 2: Implement the Library System

```java
import java.util.ArrayList;
import java.util.HashSet;
import java.util.HashMap;


public class LibrarySystem {
    private ArrayList<Book> books; // Store books
    private HashSet<String> authors; // Store unique authors
    private HashMap<Integer, Book> bookLookup; // Store books
by their ID


    public LibrarySystem() {
        books = new ArrayList<>();
        authors = new HashSet<>();
```

```java
        bookLookup = new HashMap<>();
    }

    public void addBook(Book book) {
        books.add(book);
        authors.add(book.getAuthor());
        bookLookup.put(book.getId(), book);
    }

    public void printBooks() {
        books.forEach(System.out::println);
    }

    public void printAuthors() {
        authors.forEach(System.out::println);
    }

    public Book getBookById(int id) {
        return bookLookup.get(id);
    }

    public static void main(String[] args) {
        LibrarySystem library = new LibrarySystem();

        // Add books to the library
```

```java
        library.addBook(new Book(1, "The Great Gatsby", "F. Scott
Fitzgerald"));
        library.addBook(new Book(2, "1984", "George Orwell"));
        library.addBook(new Book(3, "To Kill a Mockingbird",
"Harper Lee"));

        // Print all books
        System.out.println("Books in the Library:");
        library.printBooks();

        // Print all authors
        System.out.println("\nAuthors:");
        library.printAuthors();

        // Get a book by ID
        System.out.println("\nBook with ID 2: " +
library.getBookById(2));
    }
}
```

5. Conclusion

In this chapter, we've explored the **Java Collections Framework**, focusing on **List**, **Set**, and **Map** interfaces and their implementations. We've covered how to work with **ArrayList**, **HashSet**, and **HashMap**, as well as how to sort, filter, and manipulate data within these collections.

Through the **Library Management System** project, you gained hands-on experience using collections to store books, manage unique authors, and look up books by their IDs.

Next Steps:

- Expand your library system to include features like borrowing and returning books.

- Explore more collection types like **TreeSet** and **TreeMap**, which offer sorted collections.

- Practice working with **Streams** to process data in collections more efficiently.

Chapter 7: Exception Handling in Java

Introduction

Imagine you're building a banking application where users can check their account balances, make transfers, and view transaction histories. However, what happens when things don't go as expected? Maybe the user enters an invalid account number, tries to withdraw more money than they have, or encounters a system failure. If your program doesn't handle these situations properly, it could crash or behave unpredictably.

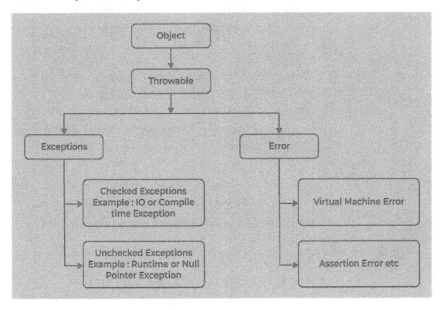

This is where **exception handling** comes in.

In this chapter, we'll dive deep into how **exception handling** works in Java. You'll learn about the types of exceptions, how to handle them using the try-catch blocks, and how to create custom exceptions for your own unique needs. By the end of this chapter, you'll have the skills to make your programs more resilient and reliable by catching and managing errors effectively.

We'll also work on a **hands-on project**: building a simple banking application that demonstrates the power of exception handling in managing **insufficient funds** and **invalid inputs**.

What You'll Need:

Before jumping into the code, let's make sure you're ready to get started:

1. **Software:**

   o **Java Development Kit (JDK)**: You should already have this installed if you've followed the previous chapters. If not, download and install it from Oracle's official website.

   o **IDE (Integrated Development Environment)**: We recommend **IntelliJ IDEA** or **Eclipse** for Java development. They offer features like auto-completion, debugging tools, and syntax highlighting, which make coding much easier.

2. **Hardware:**

   o A computer with at least **2GB of RAM** and sufficient storage space to handle your Java projects.

3. **Prerequisites:**

   o Familiarity with Java syntax, classes, and basic programming concepts. If you've followed the earlier chapters, you're already well-prepared to tackle exception handling.

1. Understanding Exceptions

An **exception** is an event that disrupts the normal flow of a program. It occurs when the program encounters an error that it cannot handle on its own, such as trying to divide by zero, accessing a file that doesn't exist, or using a null object reference.

When an exception occurs, Java creates an object (the exception) and throws it to indicate that something went wrong. If not handled properly, the program will terminate unexpectedly, leading to poor user experience and possibly data loss.

Types of Exceptions: Checked vs. Unchecked

Java exceptions can be broadly classified into two categories: **checked exceptions** and **unchecked exceptions**.

1.1 Checked Exceptions

Checked exceptions are exceptions that the **compiler requires** you to handle. These exceptions usually occur due to external factors, such as file access issues, network problems, or invalid user input.

Examples of checked exceptions:

- **IOException**: Thrown when an I/O operation fails (e.g., file not found).

- **SQLException**: Thrown when there is a database-related error.

Why handle checked exceptions?

- They represent issues that can be anticipated and are usually outside the program's immediate control (like network failures or missing files).

- If a method throws a checked exception, you must either **catch** the exception or declare it with the throws keyword.

Example: Handling a checked exception

```java
import java.io.*;

public class CheckedExceptionExample {
    public static void main(String[] args) {
        try {
            FileReader reader = new FileReader("non_existent_file.txt"); // This will throw an exception
        } catch (IOException e) {
            System.out.println("An error occurred while reading the file: " + e.getMessage());
        }
    }
}
```

1.2 Unchecked Exceptions

Unchecked exceptions are exceptions that are **not checked by the compiler**. These usually occur due to programming bugs, such as accessing null references or dividing by zero.

Examples of unchecked exceptions:

- **NullPointerException**: Occurs when trying to use an object reference that is null.

- **ArithmeticException**: Occurs when dividing by zero.

- **ArrayIndexOutOfBoundsException**: Occurs when trying to access an invalid array index.

Unlike checked exceptions, the compiler does not force you to handle unchecked exceptions. However, you should still handle them appropriately to prevent your program from crashing.

Example: Handling an unchecked exception

```
public class UncheckedExceptionExample {
    public static void main(String[] args) {
        try {
            int result = 10 / 0;  // This will throw ArithmeticException
        } catch (ArithmeticException e) {
            System.out.println("Error: Cannot divide by zero!");
        }
    }
}
```

2. The try-catch-finally Block

The try-catch block in Java is used to handle exceptions and ensure that the program doesn't terminate abruptly. It allows you to catch and respond to exceptions when they occur.

- **try block**: Contains the code that might throw an exception.

- **catch block**: Catches the exception if it occurs and handles it.

- **finally block**: Contains code that will always run, regardless of whether an exception occurred. It's useful for cleaning up resources (like closing a file or database connection).

Syntax of try-catch-finally

```
try {
    // Code that may throw an exception
} catch (ExceptionType e) {
    // Code that handles the exception
```

```
} finally {

    // Code that will always run, whether an exception occurred or
not

}
```

2.1 Throw/Throws Keyword

In addition to catching exceptions, you can **throw** exceptions manually using the throw keyword. This is useful when you want to explicitly signal that something went wrong.

- **throw**: Used to explicitly throw an exception in your code.

- **throws**: Used in method declarations to indicate that a method may throw certain exceptions.

Example: Throwing an exception

```
public class ThrowExample {

    public static void checkAge(int age) {

        if (age < 18) {

            throw new IllegalArgumentException("Age must be 18 or
older");

        }

        System.out.println("Age is valid");

    }


    public static void main(String[] args) {

        try {

            checkAge(15); // This will throw an exception

        } catch (IllegalArgumentException e) {

            System.out.println("Error: " + e.getMessage());
```

```
        }
     }
}
```

In this example, if the age is less than 18, an IllegalArgumentException is thrown with a custom message.

---

3. Custom Exceptions

Sometimes, you may need to create your own exceptions to represent specific errors in your application. Java allows you to create custom exception classes by extending the Exception class (for checked exceptions) or RuntimeException (for unchecked exceptions).

3.1 How and When to Create Custom Exception Classes

Custom exceptions are useful when you need to handle specific error conditions in your application, which aren't covered by the standard Java exceptions. For instance, if you're building a banking application, you might want to create an exception for "insufficient funds."

Example: Creating a custom exception

```
public class InsufficientFundsException extends Exception {

    public InsufficientFundsException(String message) {

        super(message); // Call the parent class (Exception)
constructor

    }
}
```

You can now use this custom exception in your program, just like any other exception:

```
public class BankAccount {
```

```java
private double balance;

public BankAccount(double balance) {
    this.balance = balance;
}

public void withdraw(double amount) throws InsufficientFundsException {
    if (amount > balance) {
        throw new InsufficientFundsException("Insufficient funds for withdrawal");
    }
    balance -= amount;
    System.out.println("Withdrawal successful! New balance: " + balance);
}
}
```

In this example, the withdraw method throws an InsufficientFundsException if the withdrawal amount exceeds the account balance.

---

4. Hands-On Example: Build a Simple Banking Application

Let's now apply what we've learned by building a **Simple Banking Application**. This system will allow users to deposit, withdraw, and check their balance while handling common exceptions such as **insufficient funds** and **invalid input**.

Step 1: Define the BankAccount Class

```java
public class BankAccount {
    private double balance;

    public BankAccount(double initialBalance) {
        this.balance = initialBalance;
    }

    // Deposit method
    public void deposit(double amount) {
        if (amount > 0) {
            balance += amount;
            System.out.println("Deposit successful! New balance: " + balance);
        } else {
            System.out.println("Error: Invalid deposit amount.");
        }
    }

    // Withdraw method with exception handling
    public void withdraw(double amount) throws InsufficientFundsException {
        if (amount > balance) {
            throw new InsufficientFundsException("Insufficient funds for withdrawal");
        }
        balance -= amount;
```

```java
System.out.println("Withdrawal successful! New balance: " +
balance);
    }


    // Check balance
    public double getBalance() {
        return balance;
    }
}
```

Step 2: Define the Custom Exception (InsufficientFundsException)

```java
public class InsufficientFundsException extends Exception {
    public InsufficientFundsException(String message) {
        super(message);
    }
}
```

Step 3: Create the Main Class for Testing

```java
public class Main {
    public static void main(String[] args) {
        BankAccount account = new BankAccount(500.0);

        try {
            account.deposit(150.0);  // Valid deposit
            account.withdraw(700.0); // Will throw
InsufficientFundsException
        } catch (InsufficientFundsException e) {
```

```
        System.out.println("Error: " + e.getMessage());
    }


    System.out.println("Final balance: " + account.getBalance());
    }
}
```

5. Best Practices in Exception Handling

While exception handling is powerful, there are some best practices you should follow to avoid common pitfalls and ensure your code is both robust and maintainable.

5.1 Avoid Empty Catch Blocks

An empty catch block silently ignores exceptions, which can lead to undetected errors in your program. Always handle exceptions properly or log them for later review.

Bad Practice:

```
try {
    // Some code that might throw an exception
} catch (Exception e) {
    // Empty catch block, error is silently ignored
}
```

Good Practice:

```
try {
    // Some code that might throw an exception
} catch (Exception e) {
    System.out.println("An error occurred: " + e.getMessage());
```

```
    e.printStackTrace(); // Optionally log the stack trace for
debugging
}
```

5.2 Chaining Exceptions

When handling an exception and throwing a new one, it's a good idea to **chain exceptions**. This way, you can preserve the original exception while providing additional context.

Example of Exception Chaining:

```
try {
    // Some code that throws an exception
} catch (IOException e) {
    throw new CustomException("Error occurred during file
processing", e);
}
```

In this case, the original IOException is passed to the new CustomException, preserving the context of the error.

5.3 Logging Errors

Use logging libraries (like **Log4j** or **SLF4J**) to log exceptions, especially in production environments. This allows you to keep track of errors and analyze them later.

Conclusion

In this chapter, you learned how to handle **exceptions** in Java using the try-catch-finally block. We covered the differences between **checked** and **unchecked exceptions**, how to use the throw and throws keywords, and when to create custom exception classes.

You also gained hands-on experience building a **Simple Banking Application** that demonstrates how to handle errors such as **insufficient funds** and **invalid inputs**. Additionally, you explored

best practices for exception handling, including avoiding empty catch blocks, chaining exceptions, and logging errors.

Next Steps:

- Expand the banking application by adding additional features like transferring money between accounts or applying interest rates.

- Explore how to handle multiple exceptions at once using multi-catch blocks and creating custom exception hierarchies for more complex error handling.

By understanding and implementing proper exception handling, you'll be able to write Java applications that are resilient, maintainable, and provide a great user experience.

Chapter 8: Java Streams and Lambda Expressions

Introduction to Functional Programming in Java

Java is a versatile language, known for its object-oriented roots and wide range of applications. However, in recent years, Java has embraced functional programming, making it even more powerful and expressive. One of the key features introduced in **Java 8** to support functional programming is **Streams** and **Lambda Expressions**.

In this chapter, we'll explore how Java's Streams and Lambda Expressions can drastically improve the readability and performance of your code. These features allow you to manipulate collections of data in a more declarative and functional style, making your code cleaner, more concise, and easier to maintain.

You'll learn how to leverage **Streams** to perform operations like filtering, mapping, and reducing, and how **Lambda Expressions** make writing functional code easier and more intuitive. We'll dive into real-world examples to demonstrate how these concepts are applied in data processing, from simple transformations to more complex data analysis.

By the end of this chapter, you will understand the power of functional programming in Java, and how to use **Streams** and **Lambda Expressions** to process data more effectively.

What You'll Need:

Before we get started, let's ensure you have the necessary setup:

1. **Software:**

   o **Java Development Kit (JDK):** You should have **JDK 8** or later installed on your computer. If you haven't done so already, download it from the Oracle website.

   o **IDE (Integrated Development Environment):** We recommend using **IntelliJ IDEA** or **Eclipse** for Java development. These IDEs offer features like code suggestions, syntax highlighting, and debugging tools to make your programming experience smoother.

2. **Hardware:**

   o A computer with **at least 2GB of RAM** and sufficient storage to handle your projects.

3. **Prerequisites:**

   o Familiarity with basic Java concepts, including **collections** (List, Set, Map) and **object-oriented**

programming. If you've followed the previous chapters, you're already in good shape to dive into Streams and Lambdas.

1. The Power of Streams and Lambda Expressions in Modern Java

In earlier versions of Java, working with collections involved manually iterating over data using loops, which could often become verbose and difficult to maintain. Java 8 introduced the **Stream API** and **Lambda Expressions**, which significantly simplify and optimize how we work with collections.

What Are Streams?

A **Stream** is an abstraction that allows you to work with sequences of data in a **functional style**. Streams can process data in a **pipeline**, meaning that each operation can be chained together to form a series of steps that transform data.

Streams are **not data structures**—they do not store data. Instead, they convey a sequence of data from a source (such as a collection) to a destination (such as an output or a result).

What Are Lambda Expressions?

A **Lambda Expression** is a concise way to represent an anonymous function (a function without a name) that can be passed around. Lambda expressions enable functional-style programming in Java and are used primarily to define the behavior for the **Stream operations** like map, filter, and reduce.

Syntax of a Lambda Expression:

(parameters) -> expression

- **Example:** (x, y) -> x + y is a simple lambda expression that sums two values.

2. Working with Streams

Streams in Java allow you to process data in a series of operations, such as filtering, mapping, and reducing. These operations are very efficient and can be processed **lazily**, meaning the data is not processed until it's needed.

2.1 Stream Operations

Stream operations can be categorized into two types:

- **Intermediate Operations**: These operations return a new stream, allowing you to chain multiple operations together. Examples include filter(), map(), sorted(), and distinct().

- **Terminal Operations**: These operations produce a result or a side-effect, such as forEach(), collect(), reduce(), and count().

2.2 Performing Operations on Collections with Streams

Let's start by looking at a few common operations you can perform on a **Stream**.

Example 1: Filter and Map Operations

Let's say we have a list of employees, and we want to filter out those who are older than 30, then map their names into uppercase.

```
import java.util.*;
import java.util.stream.*;


public class StreamExample {
    public static void main(String[] args) {
        List<Employee> employees = Arrays.asList(
            new Employee("John", 25),
            new Employee("Alice", 35),
```

```java
        new Employee("Bob", 40),
        new Employee("Charlie", 29)
    );


    List<String> filteredNames = employees.stream()
        .filter(e -> e.getAge() > 30) // Filtering employees older than 30
        .map(e -> e.getName().toUpperCase()) // Mapping names to uppercase
        .collect(Collectors.toList()); // Collecting the results into a list

        filteredNames.forEach(System.out::println);
    }
}

class Employee {
    private String name;
    private int age;

    public Employee(String name, int age) {
        this.name = name;
        this.age = age;
    }

    public String getName() {
```

```
    return name;
  }

  public int getAge() {
    return age;
  }
}
```

Explanation:

- **filter():** This method filters the stream based on a given condition—in this case, it selects employees older than 30.

- **map():** This method transforms the stream elements—in this case, converting names to uppercase.

- **collect():** This terminal operation collects the results into a list.

Example 2: Sorting a Stream

We can also sort data in a stream using the sorted() method.

```
List<Employee> sortedEmployees = employees.stream()
    .sorted(Comparator.comparing(Employee::getAge)) // Sorting by age
    .collect(Collectors.toList());

sortedEmployees.forEach(e -> System.out.println(e.getName() + ": " + e.getAge()));
```

3. Understanding the Stream Pipeline

A **Stream Pipeline** is a combination of a sequence of **intermediate** and **terminal operations** that transform data in a sequence. The key feature of a stream pipeline is **laziness**: intermediate operations are not executed until a terminal operation is invoked.

Stream Pipeline Example:

```
List<String> result = employees.stream()
    .filter(e -> e.getAge() > 30)
    .map(Employee::getName)
    .sorted()
    .collect(Collectors.toList());
```

- **filter()**: Filters employees with age greater than 30.
- **map()**: Extracts the name of each employee.
- **sorted()**: Sorts the names alphabetically.
- **collect()**: Collects the names into a list.

4. Hands-On Example: Manipulate a List of Employees

Now that you have a good understanding of streams, let's put it into practice by building a **List of Employees** and applying **filtering**, **sorting**, and **mapping** operations to manipulate the data.

Step 1: Create an Employee Class

```
class Employee {
    private String name;
    private int age;
    private double salary;
```

```java
public Employee(String name, int age, double salary) {
    this.name = name;
    this.age = age;
    this.salary = salary;
}

public String getName() {
    return name;
}

public int getAge() {
    return age;
}

public double getSalary() {
    return salary;
}

@Override
public String toString() {
    return "Employee{name='" + name + "', age=" + age + ", salary="
+ salary + "}";
}
}
```

Step 2: Create a List of Employees

```
List<Employee> employees = Arrays.asList(
    new Employee("John", 25, 50000),
    new Employee("Alice", 35, 80000),
    new Employee("Bob", 40, 60000),
    new Employee("Charlie", 29, 70000)
);
```

Step 3: Perform Stream Operations

```
public class EmployeeStreamExample {
    public static void main(String[] args) {
        List<Employee> employees = Arrays.asList(
            new Employee("John", 25, 50000),
            new Employee("Alice", 35, 80000),
            new Employee("Bob", 40, 60000),
            new Employee("Charlie", 29, 70000)
        );

        // Filtering employees with salary greater than 60000
        List<Employee> highEarners = employees.stream()
            .filter(e -> e.getSalary() > 60000)
            .collect(Collectors.toList());

        highEarners.forEach(System.out::println);
    }
```

```
}
```

In this example:

- We use the filter() operation to select employees with a salary greater than $60,000.

- Then, we use collect() to gather the results into a list and print the details of each employee in the result.

---

5. Real-World Application: Data Analysis in Java

One of the most powerful uses of **Streams** and **Lambda Expressions** is in data analysis. Whether you're processing **logs**, **financial data**, or **user activity data**, these tools provide an efficient and elegant way to process large datasets.

5.1 Example: Analyzing Sales Data

Let's say we have a list of sales transactions, and we need to analyze the total sales, average sales, and find the highest-selling product.

```
import java.util. *;
import java.util.stream. *;


class Sale {
    private String product;
    private double amount;

    public Sale(String product, double amount) {
        this.product = product;
        this.amount = amount;
```

```java
    }

    public String getProduct() {
        return product;
    }

    public double getAmount() {
        return amount;
    }
}

public class SalesDataAnalysis {
    public static void main(String[] args) {
        List<Sale> sales = Arrays.asList(
            new Sale("Laptop", 1000),
            new Sale("Phone", 700),
            new Sale("Tablet", 400),
            new Sale("Laptop", 1200),
            new Sale("Phone", 800)
        );

        // Total sales
        double totalSales = sales.stream()
            .mapToDouble(Sale::getAmount)
            .sum();
```

```
// Average sales
double averageSales = sales.stream()
    .mapToDouble(Sale::getAmount)
    .average()
    .orElse(0);

// Highest selling product
Optional<Sale> maxSale = sales.stream()
    .max(Comparator.comparingDouble(Sale::getAmount));

System.out.println("Total Sales: " + totalSales);
System.out.println("Average Sales: " + averageSales);
maxSale.ifPresent(sale -> System.out.println("Highest Selling
Product: " + sale.getProduct()));
    }
}
```

In this example:

- **mapToDouble(Sale::getAmount)** is used to extract the sale amounts for calculation.

- **sum()** and **average()** are terminal operations that return the total and average sales.

- **max()** finds the highest sale.

Conclusion

In this chapter, you learned how **Java Streams** and **Lambda Expressions** provide powerful tools for data manipulation in modern Java. Streams allow you to process collections in a functional style, while Lambda Expressions make it easier to define behavior concisely and readably.

Through examples like **filtering employees**, **sorting data**, and performing **data analysis on sales transactions**, you've seen how these tools can simplify complex data processing tasks.

Next Steps:

- Experiment with other stream operations like **flatMap()** and **distinct()**.

- Try applying streams and lambda expressions to analyze different types of data, such as **financial records, user logs**, or **product reviews**.

With your newfound understanding of Java Streams and Lambda Expressions, you are now equipped to process and analyze data efficiently in your applications, making your code more readable and maintainable.

Chapter 9: Building Cross-Platform Apps with JavaFX

Introduction to JavaFX

JavaFX is a powerful framework for building rich, interactive graphical user interfaces (GUIs) in Java. With JavaFX, you can develop **cross-platform desktop applications** that run on Windows, macOS, and Linux. It is Java's modern alternative to the older Swing framework, providing enhanced features for creating engaging user interfaces.

In this chapter, we will dive into how JavaFX allows you to create applications with visually appealing interfaces and smooth, interactive experiences. We will start by introducing you to the core concepts of JavaFX, including the JavaFX **Application Thread**, and then proceed to work with basic JavaFX components like **Stage, Scene, Button, TextField, VBox**, and **HBox**.

We'll then dive into a **hands-on project**, where you'll learn how to build a **To-Do List Application**. This project will allow you to apply your newfound JavaFX skills by creating a user-friendly interface to add, remove, and complete tasks. Finally, we will explore **advanced JavaFX features**, including animations, event handling, and managing complex layouts, to further enhance your app.

What You'll Need

Before jumping into the code, let's make sure you're ready:

1. **Software:**

   o **Java Development Kit (JDK):** If you don't already have it, download and install **JDK 8 or later** from Oracle's website.

- o **JavaFX SDK**: You'll need the **JavaFX SDK** for building JavaFX applications. This is available for download from the OpenJFX website.

- o **IDE (Integrated Development Environment)**: We recommend **IntelliJ IDEA** or **Eclipse** for a smooth development experience. Make sure your IDE has support for JavaFX (in IntelliJ IDEA, this support is built-in).

- o **Maven or Gradle** (Optional): For managing JavaFX dependencies in larger projects, tools like Maven or Gradle can help handle the setup.

2. **Hardware:**

- o A computer with **at least 2GB of RAM** and enough storage to run Java and your project files.

3. **Prerequisites:**

- o Basic knowledge of **Java syntax** and **object-oriented programming** concepts. If you've followed previous chapters, you're already familiar with Java's basics, so you should be ready to dive into JavaFX.

1. Understanding JavaFX: The Basics

JavaFX provides a rich set of **UI components** and **APIs** for building cross-platform applications. The fundamental building blocks of a JavaFX application include:

- **Stage**: The top-level container for your application, similar to a window.

- **Scene**: The content inside a stage. A scene contains all the elements you want to display on the screen, such as buttons, text fields, and labels.

- **Controls and Layouts**: These are the interactive components (e.g., buttons, text fields) and the containers that help organize these components (e.g., VBox, HBox).

1.1 The JavaFX Application Thread

JavaFX applications are single-threaded, and all UI-related updates must be done on the **JavaFX Application Thread**. This is a special thread dedicated to handling GUI updates. If you try to update the UI from a background thread (such as when performing I/O operations or long-running tasks), you'll encounter errors or unexpected behavior.

To update the UI from another thread, you must use the Platform.runLater() method, which ensures that the update happens on the JavaFX Application Thread.

2. Basic JavaFX Components

Let's break down some of the core JavaFX components you'll work with to build your first GUI application.

2.1 Stage and Scene

In JavaFX, the **Stage** is the top-level container (like a window), and the **Scene** contains the UI elements (buttons, labels, text fields, etc.) that will be displayed in the window.

- A **Stage** represents a window.

- A **Scene** is the content inside the Stage.

Example: Creating a Stage and Scene

```
import javafx.application.Application;

import javafx.scene.Scene;

import javafx.scene.control.Button;

import javafx.stage.Stage;
```

```java
public class SimpleApp extends Application {

    @Override
    public void start(Stage primaryStage) {
        // Creating a button
        Button btn = new Button("Click Me");

        // Setting up the scene with the button
        Scene scene = new Scene(btn, 300, 200);

        // Setting the title of the stage
        primaryStage.setTitle("JavaFX Example");

        // Setting the scene for the stage
        primaryStage.setScene(scene);

        // Displaying the stage
        primaryStage.show();
    }

    public static void main(String[] args) {
        launch(args);
    }
}
```

Here, the start() method is where you create the **Stage** and **Scene**. A Button is added to the scene, and the scene is then displayed on the stage.

2.2 Basic UI Controls: Button, TextField, and Labels

JavaFX provides a wide variety of UI controls. The most commonly used ones include:

- **Button**: Used for user interaction.

- **TextField**: A field for user input.

- **Label**: A simple text component.

Example: Button and TextField

```java
import javafx.application.Application;
import javafx.scene.Scene;
import javafx.scene.control.Button;
import javafx.scene.control.TextField;
import javafx.stage.Stage;

public class ButtonTextFieldExample extends Application {

    @Override
    public void start(Stage primaryStage) {
        // Create UI components
        TextField textField = new TextField();
        Button button = new Button("Submit");
```

```
button.setOnAction(e -> System.out.println("Text entered: " +
textField.getText()));

        // Setting up the layout
        VBox layout = new VBox(10);
        layout.getChildren().addAll(textField, button);

        // Set up the scene
        Scene scene = new Scene(layout, 300, 200);

        // Set up the stage
        primaryStage.setTitle("Button and TextField Example");
        primaryStage.setScene(scene);
        primaryStage.show();
    }

    public static void main(String[] args) {
        launch(args);
    }
}
```

In this example:

- A **TextField** is used to get input from the user.

- A **Button** is set to print the text entered in the **TextField** when clicked.

2.3 Layouts: VBox and HBox

To organize your UI components, JavaFX provides **layout managers** like **VBox** and **HBox**:

- **VBox** arranges components vertically.

- **HBox** arranges components horizontally.

Example: Using VBox and HBox

```
import javafx.application.Application;
import javafx.scene.Scene;
import javafx.scene.control.Button;
import javafx.scene.layout.HBox;
import javafx.stage.Stage;


public class LayoutExample extends Application {


    @Override
    public void start(Stage primaryStage) {
        // Create buttons
        Button button1 = new Button("Button 1");
        Button button2 = new Button("Button 2");


        // Use HBox to arrange buttons horizontally
        HBox layout = new HBox(10);  // 10px spacing
        layout.getChildren().addAll(button1, button2);


        // Set up the scene
```

```
    Scene scene = new Scene(layout, 300, 200);

    // Set up the stage
    primaryStage.setTitle("HBox Example");
    primaryStage.setScene(scene);
    primaryStage.show();
    }

    public static void main(String[] args) {
        launch(args);
    }
}
```

3. Hands-On Project: Build a To-Do List Application

Now that you've learned about JavaFX components, let's build a **To-Do List Application** to apply these concepts.

In this project, we will:

- Use a **ListView** to display tasks.

- Provide **TextField** for adding new tasks.

- Use **Button** to add tasks, remove tasks, and mark tasks as completed.

- Organize components with **VBox** and **HBox**.

Step 1: Create the To-Do List Application

```java
import javafx.application.Application;
import javafx.collections.FXCollections;
import javafx.collections.ObservableList;
import javafx.scene.Scene;
import javafx.scene.control.*;
import javafx.scene.layout.*;
import javafx.stage.Stage;


public class TodoApp extends Application {

    @Override
    public void start(Stage primaryStage) {
        // Create the task list
        ObservableList<String> tasks =
FXCollections.observableArrayList();

        // ListView to display tasks
        ListView<String> listView = new ListView<>(tasks);
        listView.setEditable(true);

        // TextField for adding new tasks
        TextField taskInput = new TextField();
        taskInput.setPromptText("Enter a task...");

        // Button to add a task
```

```java
Button addButton = new Button("Add Task");
addButton.setOnAction(e -> {
    String task = taskInput.getText();
    if (!task.isEmpty()) {
        tasks.add(task);
        taskInput.clear();
    }
});


// Button to remove selected task
Button removeButton = new Button("Remove Task");
removeButton.setOnAction(e -> {
    String selectedTask =
listView.getSelectionModel().getSelectedItem();
    if (selectedTask != null) {
        tasks.remove(selectedTask);
    }
});


// Layout the components
VBox layout = new VBox(10);
HBox inputLayout = new HBox(10);
inputLayout.getChildren().addAll(taskInput, addButton);
layout.getChildren().addAll(inputLayout, listView,
removeButton);
```

```
// Set up the scene
Scene scene = new Scene(layout, 400, 300);
primaryStage.setTitle("To-Do List Application");
primaryStage.setScene(scene);
primaryStage.show();
}


public static void main(String[] args) {
    launch(args);
}
}
```

4. JavaFX Advanced Features

Once you have a working application, you can enhance it with more advanced features. Some of these features include **animations**, **event handling**, and managing more **complex layouts**.

4.1 Animations in JavaFX

JavaFX provides a powerful **animation API** that allows you to animate UI components. For example, you can create simple animations like moving a button, changing its size, or fading it in/out.

Example: Animating a Button

```
Scene scene = new Scene(root, 300, 250);
primaryStage.setTitle("Button Animation");
primaryStage.setScene(scene);
primaryStage.show();
}
```

```java
    public static void main(String[] args) {
        launch(args);
    }
}
import javafx.animation.*;
import javafx.application.Application;
import javafx.scene.Scene;
import javafx.scene.control.Button;
import javafx.scene.layout.StackPane;
import javafx.stage.Stage;
import javafx.util.Duration;

public class ButtonAnimationExample extends Application {

    @Override
    public void start(Stage primaryStage) {
        Button btn = new Button("Click me!");

        // Create an animation that moves the button
        TranslateTransition transition = new TranslateTransition();
        transition.setNode(btn);
        transition.setToX(200);
        transition.setToY(100);
        transition.setCycleCount(TranslateTransition.INDEFINITE);
```

```
transition.setAutoReverse(true);
transition.setDuration(Duration.seconds(2));

btn.setOnAction(e -> transition.play());

StackPane root = new StackPane();
root.getChildren().add(btn);
```

4.2 Event Handling in JavaFX

JavaFX provides an easy way to handle user interactions through event handling. You can listen for various events like **mouse clicks, key presses, window resizing**, and much more.

Example: Handling Mouse Click Events

```
Button btn = new Button("Click Me!");
btn.setOnMouseClicked(e -> {
    System.out.println("Button clicked!");
});
```

4.3 Managing Complex Layouts

JavaFX provides several layout managers, including **BorderPane, GridPane**, and **FlowPane**, to help you create complex, responsive interfaces.

Example: Using GridPane for Layout

```
GridPane grid = new GridPane();
grid.setHgap(10);
```

```
grid.setVgap(10);

TextField textField = new TextField();
Button button = new Button("Submit");

grid.add(textField, 0, 0);
grid.add(button, 1, 0);

Scene scene = new Scene(grid, 300, 250);
primaryStage.setTitle("Grid Layout");
primaryStage.setScene(scene);
primaryStage.show();
```

Conclusion

In this chapter, we explored **JavaFX** and how to create **cross-platform applications** with powerful, interactive **user interfaces**. You learned how to:

- Work with **Stage, Scene,** and **UI components** like **Button, TextField,** and **Label.**

- Use **VBox** and **HBox** for organizing your UI elements in a flexible layout.

- Build a **To-Do List Application** as a hands-on project, demonstrating how to handle basic operations like adding, removing, and completing tasks.

- Dive deeper into **advanced JavaFX features,** including animations, event handling, and more complex layouts.

JavaFX gives you the tools to create rich, interactive desktop applications that can run on multiple platforms. Now, you can take your skills even further by adding more advanced features to your applications and experimenting with custom layouts, event handling, and animations.

Chapter 10: Developing Mobile Apps with Java (Android)

Introduction to Android Development with Java

As the mobile industry continues to evolve, the demand for powerful, feature-rich apps remains high. For developers, Android is one of the most popular platforms to target, and Java has been the cornerstone of Android development for years. Even though Kotlin has become a first-class language for Android development, **Java** continues to be the go-to language for building robust, cross-platform Android applications.

In this chapter, we will guide you through the essentials of developing mobile applications using Java for Android. From setting up the development environment to building your first simple app, this chapter will provide all the foundation you need to get started in the world of mobile app development.

We will also walk you through building a **Basic Calculator App** using Java for Android. This hands-on project will help you gain experience working with Android's layout system, user interface (UI) components, and simple logic.

What You'll Need:

Before diving into Android development, ensure you have everything set up:

1. **Software:**

   - **Android Studio**: Android Studio is the official integrated development environment (IDE) for Android development. You can download it from here.

   - **Java Development Kit (JDK)**: You should have **JDK 8 or later** installed. It comes with Android Studio, so if you've already installed it, you're good to go.

   - **Android SDK**: The Android SDK comes bundled with Android Studio, which allows you to develop and test Android apps.

   - **Emulator or Physical Device**: For testing your apps, you can use either an Android emulator (provided by Android Studio) or a physical Android device. Make sure to enable **USB debugging** on your Android device if you want to test on a real device.

2. **Hardware:**

   o   A computer with at least **2GB of RAM** (8GB is preferred) and enough storage to run Android Studio and your Android projects.

3. **Prerequisites:**

   o   Basic knowledge of Java, object-oriented programming, and understanding basic concepts like variables, loops, and conditionals.

   o   Familiarity with the Android platform's basic components (e.g., activities, layouts, and views) will be helpful but is not required.

---

1. Why Java is Still the Go-To Language for Android Development

Java remains the primary programming language for Android development for several reasons:

1. **Cross-Platform Compatibility**: Java is a platform-independent language, meaning Java applications can run on any device that supports Java. This is particularly useful in the Android ecosystem, where devices have varying specifications and screen sizes.

2. **Rich Libraries and Frameworks**: Java has a robust set of libraries and frameworks that make app development faster and more efficient. The **Android SDK** (Software Development

Kit) provides everything you need to develop Android apps, and most of it is written in Java.

3. **Community and Support**: Java has a large and active community of developers, ensuring plenty of resources like forums, tutorials, and documentation. Android's support for Java remains strong, making it easier for developers to get help when needed.

4. **Backward Compatibility**: Java has been around for a long time, and many legacy Android applications and frameworks are built using Java. It allows developers to maintain and improve older apps alongside new ones.

2. Setting Up Android Studio and Understanding Android Components

Before we start coding, let's set up **Android Studio** and understand some of the basic Android components.

2.1 Setting Up Android Studio

1. **Download and Install Android Studio**:

    o   Go to Android Studio's official download page and download the installer for your operating system.

    o   Follow the installation instructions on the website.

2. **Setting Up the Android SDK**:

    o   Android Studio automatically installs the Android SDK, but during the installation, you'll be asked to download the required SDK components.

o   Once Android Studio is set up, you'll be able to download various SDK tools and versions to target specific Android versions for your app.

3. **Setting Up the Emulator**:

o   To test your app, you can either use a physical Android device or set up an **Android Virtual Device (AVD)** via Android Studio's AVD Manager. The emulator simulates different Android devices, allowing you to test apps without needing a physical device.

2.2 Basic Android Components

Android apps are built using a few essential components:

- **Activities**: These represent individual screens in your app. Each activity is a separate screen that interacts with the user. For example, a login screen, a dashboard, or a settings screen.

- **Views**: Views are the UI components that make up the layout of your screen. These include buttons, text fields, and images.

- **Layouts**: Layouts are used to organize views. Examples include LinearLayout, RelativeLayout, ConstraintLayout, etc.

3. Creating Your First Android App

Let's create a simple "**Hello World**" Android app. This app will serve as your first step toward understanding the structure of an Android app and the relationship between the **Activity**, **UI Components**, and **Layouts**.

3.1 Creating a New Android Project

1. **Launch Android Studio** and click on **Start a new Android Studio project**.

2. Choose the **Empty Activity** template (this gives you a simple starting point).

3. Set the **name** of the project (e.g., "HelloWorldApp") and the **language** to **Java**.

4. Choose the **minimum API level** (for beginners, you can choose API 21 or higher).

5. Click **Finish** and wait for Android Studio to set up your project.

3.2 Understanding the Project Structure

When your project is set up, Android Studio creates the following important folders and files:

- **src/main/java/**: This folder contains the Java files, including your activity classes.

- **src/main/res/**: This folder contains resources like layouts, drawables, and strings.

- **AndroidManifest.xml**: This file defines essential information about your app, such as the activity, permissions, and API level.

3.3 Writing Your First "Hello World" App

In Android, **activities** represent individual screens. Let's modify the default MainActivity.java to display a simple text on the screen.

MainActivity.java:

```
package com.example.helloworldapp;


import android.os.Bundle;
import androidx.appcompat.app.AppCompatActivity;
import android.widget.TextView;


public class MainActivity extends AppCompatActivity {

    @Override
    protected void onCreate(Bundle savedInstanceState) {
        super.onCreate(savedInstanceState);
        setContentView(R.layout.activity_main);


        // Create a TextView and set it to display "Hello World!"
        TextView textView = new TextView(this);
        textView.setText("Hello World!");
        textView.setTextSize(30);
        setContentView(textView); // Set the TextView as the content
of the activity
    }
}
```

activity_main.xml: This is where you define the layout. For now, it can remain empty or have a simple button or text field.

<?xml version="1.0" encoding="utf-8"?>

<RelativeLayout
xmlns:android="http://schemas.android.com/apk/res/android"

  android:layout_width="match_parent"

  android:layout_height="match_parent">

  <TextView

    android:id="@+id/helloText"

    android:layout_width="wrap_content"

    android:layout_height="wrap_content"

    android:text="Hello World!"

    android:textSize="24sp"

    android:layout_centerInParent="true" />

</RelativeLayout>

1. **Run Your App**:

   o Once the code is written, press **Run** in Android Studio and select the emulator or your physical device.

   o The app should display "Hello World!" on the screen.

---

4. Hands-On Example: Build a Basic Calculator App for Android

Now that you've built your first app, let's dive into a more interactive project: a **Basic Calculator App**. In this app, we will implement simple arithmetic functions (addition, subtraction, multiplication, and division) and display the results.

4.1 Set Up the Layout for the Calculator

activity_main.xml:

```xml
<?xml version="1.0" encoding="utf-8"?>
<LinearLayout
xmlns:android="http://schemas.android.com/apk/res/android"
    android:layout_width="match_parent"
    android:layout_height="match_parent"
    android:orientation="vertical"
    android:padding="16dp">

    <!-- Display the result -->
    <TextView
        android:id="@+id/display"
        android:layout_width="match_parent"
        android:layout_height="wrap_content"
        android:text="0"
        android:textSize="36sp"
        android:textAlignment="center"
        android:layout_marginBottom="20dp" />

    <!-- Buttons for digits and operations -->
    <GridLayout
        android:layout_width="match_parent"
        android:layout_height="wrap_content"
```

```
android:columnCount="4"
android:rowCount="5">


    <Button android:id="@+id/button1" android:text="1"
style="@style/ButtonStyle" />
    <Button android:id="@+id/button2" android:text="2"
style="@style/ButtonStyle" />
    <Button android:id="@+id/button3" android:text="3"
style="@style/ButtonStyle" />
    <Button android:id="@+id/buttonAdd" android:text="+"
style="@style/ButtonStyle" />


    <!-- Repeat for other buttons (4-9, 0, =, etc.) -->


    </GridLayout>
</LinearLayout>
```

4.2 Writing the Logic for the Calculator

2. MainActivity.java:

```
package com.example.calculatorapp;


import android.os.Bundle;
import android.view.View;
import android.widget.Button;
import android.widget.TextView;
import androidx.appcompat.app.AppCompatActivity;
```

```java
public class MainActivity extends AppCompatActivity {

    private TextView display;
    private String currentInput = "";

    @Override
    protected void onCreate(Bundle savedInstanceState) {
        super.onCreate(savedInstanceState);
        setContentView(R.layout.activity_main);

        display = findViewById(R.id.display);

        // Set up button listeners
        setUpButtonListeners();
    }

    private void setUpButtonListeners() {
        // Numbers
        findViewById(R.id.button1).setOnClickListener(v ->
appendToDisplay("1"));
        findViewById(R.id.button2).setOnClickListener(v ->
appendToDisplay("2"));
        // Repeat for other number buttons...

        // Operations
```

```java
        findViewById(R.id.buttonAdd).setOnClickListener(v ->
appendToDisplay("+"));
        // Repeat for other operation buttons...


        // Equals button
        findViewById(R.id.buttonEquals).setOnClickListener(v ->
calculateResult());
    }


    private void appendToDisplay(String value) {
        currentInput += value;
        display.setText(currentInput);
    }


    private void calculateResult() {
        try {
            // Simple evaluation (could use a proper expression parser
here)
            double result = evaluateExpression(currentInput);
            display.setText(String.valueOf(result));
        } catch (Exception e) {
            display.setText("Error");
        }
    }


    private double evaluateExpression(String expression) {
```

```
    // Simple method to evaluate expressions (for demo purposes,
replace with real parser)
    // Example: Implementing basic operations using eval or
manual parsing.
    return 0; // For now, just return 0
  }
}
```

5. Java Advanced Features in Android

5.1 Event Handling in Android

Android uses **event listeners** to handle user interactions. The OnClickListener is commonly used for buttons, but Android supports various other listeners (e.g., OnTouchListener, OnKeyListener) for more complex interactions.

5.2 Working with Animations

Android provides a rich set of tools for animations, including **property animations** and **view animations**. You can animate buttons, text fields, and other UI components to create a more engaging experience.

Example: Simple Fade Animation

```
ObjectAnimator fadeOut = ObjectAnimator.ofFloat(button, "alpha",
1f, 0f);
fadeOut.setDuration(1000);
fadeOut.start();
```

Conclusion

In this chapter, we explored the essentials of Android development using Java. We covered:

- Setting up **Android Studio** and understanding **Android components** like **activities**, **views**, and **layouts**.

- Building a simple "**Hello World**" app and understanding its structure.

- Developing a **Basic Calculator App** to practice handling user input, performing arithmetic functions, and updating the UI.

- Exploring advanced features like **animations**, **event handling**, and building interactive UIs.

Now that you've laid the groundwork, you can take your knowledge and start building more complex mobile apps. Continue experimenting with additional Android features, such as **databases**, **networking**, and **background services**, to further enhance your apps.

Next Steps:

- Expand the calculator app by adding more features (e.g., scientific functions, memory functionality).

- Dive deeper into Android development by exploring more advanced topics like **custom views**, **notifications**, and **services**.

By building on these fundamentals, you're well on your way to becoming proficient in Android development with Java!

Chapter 11: Understanding Java Design Patterns

Introduction to Design Patterns

When building software systems, developers often encounter recurring problems that require similar solutions. To help solve these problems more efficiently and in a standardized way, **design patterns** were created. These patterns represent tried-and-tested solutions that can be reused across different projects, making code easier to understand, maintain, and extend.

In this chapter, we will explore **design patterns** in Java, focusing on three common patterns: the **Singleton, Factory,** and **Observer** patterns. We'll cover what each pattern is, when to use it, and how to implement it in Java. Additionally, we'll build a hands-on project to demonstrate the application of the **Singleton pattern**.

What You'll Need:

Before diving into design patterns, make sure you have the following ready:

1. **Software:**

    o **Java Development Kit (JDK):** You should already have **JDK 8 or later** installed. If not, download it from Oracle's website.

    o **IDE (Integrated Development Environment):** We recommend **IntelliJ IDEA** or **Eclipse** for Java development. These IDEs have built-in tools to help with code navigation, debugging, and project management.

2. **Hardware:**

   o A computer with at least **2GB of RAM** and enough storage to handle your Java projects.

3. **Prerequisites:**

   o Familiarity with Java syntax, object-oriented programming, and basic programming concepts such as classes, objects, inheritance, and polymorphism.

---

1. What Are Design Patterns?

A **design pattern** is a general repeatable solution to a commonly occurring problem in software design. Design patterns are like blueprints that can be customized to solve a particular design problem in your code. They help you solve complex design issues while improving the maintainability, flexibility, and scalability of your software.

Design patterns are typically categorized into three types:

1. **Creational Patterns**: Concerned with object creation mechanisms, trying to create objects in a manner suitable to the situation. Examples: **Singleton, Factory, Abstract Factory, Builder**, and **Prototype**.

2. **Structural Patterns**: Deal with object composition, creating relationships between objects to form larger structures. Examples: **Adapter, Decorator, Composite**, and **Facade**.

3. **Behavioral Patterns**: Focus on communication between objects, what goes on between objects and how they interact. Examples: **Observer**, **Strategy**, **Command**, and **State**.

In this chapter, we will focus on **Creational Patterns** (like **Singleton** and **Factory**) and **Behavioral Patterns** (like **Observer**).

---

2. Common Design Patterns and Their Use Cases

Let's dive into some of the most commonly used design patterns in Java.

2.1 Singleton Pattern

The **Singleton pattern** ensures that a class has only one instance and provides a global point of access to that instance. This pattern is useful when you need to limit the number of instances of a class, such as when you want to have only one instance of a **Logger**, **Database Connection**, or **Configuration Manager**.

When to Use Singleton Pattern:

- You need to ensure a class has only one instance (e.g., configuration class, logger).

- You need to control the instantiation of the class to maintain global state.

Example of Singleton Pattern:

```java
public class Logger {
    // Step 1: Create a private static instance of the class
    private static Logger instance;
```

```
// Step 2: Make the constructor private to prevent instantiation
private Logger() {}

// Step 3: Provide a public static method to access the instance
public static Logger getInstance() {
    if (instance == null) {
        instance = new Logger();
    }
    return instance;
}

public void log(String message) {
    System.out.println("Log: " + message);
}
}
```

In this example:

- The Logger class has a private static instance.

- The constructor is private, so it cannot be instantiated directly.

- The getInstance() method provides access to the instance, ensuring that only one instance of the Logger class is created.

2.2 Factory Pattern

The **Factory pattern** defines an interface for creating objects, but it allows subclasses to alter the type of objects that will be created. The Factory pattern helps in managing and maintaining a large number of related objects, especially when you want to hide the object creation logic from the client.

When to Use Factory Pattern:

- When the creation logic of an object is complex or needs to be abstracted.

- When you need to return different types of objects based on conditions (e.g., user input, configuration).

Example of Factory Pattern:

```java
// Product Interface
interface Product {
    void create();
}


// Concrete Product A
class ProductA implements Product {
    @Override
    public void create() {
        System.out.println("ProductA created");
    }
}


// Concrete Product B
```

```
class ProductB implements Product {
    @Override
    public void create() {
        System.out.println("ProductB created");
    }
}
```

```
// Factory Class
class ProductFactory {
    public static Product getProduct(String type) {
        if (type.equalsIgnoreCase("A")) {
            return new ProductA();
        } else if (type.equalsIgnoreCase("B")) {
            return new ProductB();
        }
        return null;
    }
}
```

In this example:

- The Product interface defines the common method create() for all products.

- The ProductFactory class decides which product to create based on the input (in this case, "A" or "B").

Usage:

```
public class FactoryPatternExample {
```

```
public static void main(String[] args) {
    Product productA = ProductFactory.getProduct("A");
    productA.create(); // Output: ProductA created

    Product productB = ProductFactory.getProduct("B");
    productB.create(); // Output: ProductB created
    }
}
```

2.3 Observer Pattern

The **Observer pattern** is used when one object (the **subject**) needs to notify other objects (the **observers**) about changes in its state. This is useful in event-driven systems, where you want multiple parts of your application to react to changes in the system state.

When to Use Observer Pattern:

- You need to notify multiple objects when a single object changes its state.

- You want to create an event-driven system where the components react to different events.

Example of Observer Pattern:

```
import java.util.*;

// Subject
class Subject {
    private List<Observer> observers = new ArrayList<>();
```

```
public void addObserver(Observer observer) {
    observers.add(observer);
}

public void removeObserver(Observer observer) {
    observers.remove(observer);
}

public void notifyObservers() {
    for (Observer observer : observers) {
        observer.update();
    }
}
}

// Observer
interface Observer {
    void update();
}

// Concrete Observer
class ConcreteObserver implements Observer {
    private String name;
```

```java
public ConcreteObserver(String name) {
    this.name = name;
}

@Override
public void update() {
    System.out.println(name + " has been notified!");
}
}
```

In this example:

- Subject manages a list of observers and notifies them of any changes.
- ConcreteObserver implements the Observer interface and performs an action when notified.

Usage:

```java
public class ObserverPatternExample {
    public static void main(String[] args) {
        // Create subject
        Subject subject = new Subject();

        // Create observers
        Observer observer1 = new ConcreteObserver("Observer1");
        Observer observer2 = new ConcreteObserver("Observer2");

        // Add observers to subject
```

```
    subject.addObserver(observer1);
    subject.addObserver(observer2);

        // Notify all observers
        subject.notifyObservers();
    }
}
```

Output:

Observer1 has been notified!

Observer2 has been notified!

---

3. Hands-On Example: Build a Simple Logging System

In this section, we will implement a simple logging system using the **Singleton pattern**. This system will ensure that only one instance of the Logger class exists, regardless of how many times it is requested.

3.1 Build the Logger Class Using Singleton Pattern

```
public class Logger {
    private static Logger instance;

    private Logger() {}

    public static Logger getInstance() {
        if (instance == null) {
            instance = new Logger();
```

```
        }
    return instance;
    }

    public void log(String message) {
        System.out.println(message);
    }
}
```

3.2 Testing the Singleton Logger

```
public class LoggerTest {
    public static void main(String[] args) {
        Logger logger1 = Logger.getInstance();
        logger1.log("First log entry");

        Logger logger2 = Logger.getInstance();
        logger2.log("Second log entry");

        // Check if both logger instances are the same
        System.out.println("Are both logger instances the same? " +
(logger1 == logger2));
    }
}
```

Output:

First log entry

Second log entry

Are both logger instances the same? true

In this example, the Logger class ensures that only one instance is created, regardless of how many times getInstance() is called.

---

4. Best Practices for Using Design Patterns in Real-World Projects

While design patterns are powerful tools for software development, they should be used judiciously. Here are some best practices to keep in mind:

4.1 When to Use Design Patterns

Design patterns should be used when:

- The problem you are solving has been encountered and solved before.

- You need a **reusable** solution that is easy to maintain and extend.

- Your project requires **scalability**, flexibility, or modularity.

4.2 Avoid Overuse of Design Patterns

- Not every situation requires a design pattern. Using patterns just for the sake of it can add unnecessary complexity to your project.

- Use design patterns only when they fit the problem. Avoid applying patterns when simple solutions work better.

4.3 Maintain Simplicity

Design patterns often make code more **robust** and **flexible**, but they can also make it **more complex**. Strive for a balance between using patterns and keeping the code simple and understandable.

Conclusion

In this chapter, we explored the concept of **design patterns** in Java and their importance in software development. We discussed three of the most commonly used design patterns: **Singleton, Factory, and Observer,** and demonstrated how to implement these patterns in Java.

Through the hands-on project of building a **Logger class** using the **Singleton pattern**, you learned how to ensure only one instance of a class is created and how to apply this pattern in real-world applications. We also discussed best practices for using design patterns, emphasizing the need to balance **flexibility** with **simplicity**.

As you continue to develop your software projects, you can apply these design patterns to improve the **maintainability, scalability, and flexibility** of your code.

Chapter 12: Working with Databases in Java (JDBC)

Introduction to JDBC (Java Database Connectivity)

In modern software development, working with databases is a critical skill. Relational databases, such as MySQL, PostgreSQL, and SQLite, are the backbone of data storage in many applications. In Java, we interact with these databases through a technology known as **JDBC** (Java Database Connectivity). JDBC allows Java applications to execute SQL queries, retrieve data, and perform other database operations in a standardized way.

This chapter will guide you through the process of working with databases in Java using JDBC. We will start by understanding how JDBC works, setting up a connection to a database, and performing **CRUD operations** (Create, Read, Update, Delete). We will also work on a **hands-on project** where we build a simple **Inventory Management System** that interacts with a MySQL database.

By the end of this chapter, you will have the knowledge to:

- Understand JDBC and how it interacts with relational databases.

- Set up JDBC and connect to a database.

- Perform CRUD operations using JDBC.

- Build a simple inventory system that stores and retrieves data from a database.

What You'll Need:

Before diving into JDBC and the Inventory Management System, ensure you have the following:

1. **Software:**

    o **Java Development Kit (JDK):** You should have **JDK 8 or later** installed. If not, download it from <u>Oracle's website</u>.

    o **MySQL** or **PostgreSQL**: You will need a running instance of a relational database. You can download MySQL from <u>here</u>, or PostgreSQL from <u>here</u>.

    o **JDBC Driver for MySQL**: You need the JDBC driver (also known as the MySQL Connector) for MySQL to connect to your database. You can download it from <u>here</u>.

    o **IDE (Integrated Development Environment):** We recommend **IntelliJ IDEA** or **Eclipse** for Java development. These IDEs make it easy to write, run, and manage Java code.

2. **Hardware:**

    o A computer with **at least 2GB of RAM** and sufficient storage to run Java and the database.

3. **Prerequisites:**

    o Basic knowledge of Java programming (variables, control flow, classes, and objects).

    o Familiarity with relational databases and SQL queries (such as SELECT, INSERT, UPDATE, and DELETE).

1. Understanding JDBC (Java Database Connectivity)

JDBC is an API that allows Java programs to interact with relational databases. It provides a standard interface for connecting to databases, executing SQL queries, and processing results. JDBC is part of the Java Standard Library, so it's available in any Java application without needing external libraries (except the database driver).

JDBC Architecture:

JDBC works in a **client-server** model:

- **Client**: The Java application that sends SQL queries to the database.

- **JDBC Driver**: A specific driver that allows Java to communicate with the database (e.g., MySQL Connector/J).

- **Database**: The relational database that stores the data.

JDBC Steps:

1. **Load the JDBC Driver**: The first step in using JDBC is loading the database driver.

2. **Establish a Connection**: You use the DriverManager.getConnection() method to establish a connection to the database.

3. **Create a Statement**: A Statement object is used to execute SQL queries.

4. **Execute SQL Queries**: You can execute queries like SELECT, INSERT, UPDATE, and DELETE.

5. **Process the Results**: The results of a query are stored in a ResultSet, which you can iterate over.

6. **Close the Connection**: It's important to close the Connection and Statement objects to free up database resources.

---

2. Setting Up JDBC and Connecting to a Database

Let's start by setting up a connection to a **MySQL** database using JDBC.

2.1 Setting Up MySQL Database

1. **Install MySQL**: If you haven't already installed MySQL, follow the instructions on the MySQL installation page.

2. **Create a Database**: After installing MySQL, you can create a database by running the following command in MySQL's command-line tool or MySQL Workbench:

CREATE DATABASE inventory_db;

Create a Table: *Inside the inventory_db database, create a table for storing inventory items:*

USE inventory_db;

CREATE TABLE inventory (

   id INT PRIMARY KEY AUTO_INCREMENT,

   name VARCHAR(255) NOT NULL,

   quantity INT NOT NULL,

   price DECIMAL(10, 2) NOT NULL

);

2.2 Adding the JDBC Driver to Your Project

For JDBC to work, you need to add the MySQL JDBC driver to your project. If you are using Maven, add the following dependency to your pom.xml:

```xml
<dependency>
    <groupId>mysql</groupId>
    <artifactId>mysql-connector-java</artifactId>
    <version>8.0.26</version>
</dependency>
```

For **Eclipse** or **IntelliJ IDEA**, you can download the **MySQL Connector/J** from here and add it to your project's build path.

3. CRUD Operations with JDBC

Now let's dive into performing **CRUD operations** (Create, Read, Update, Delete) on the inventory table using JDBC.

3.1 Create Operation (INSERT)

Let's start by inserting a new record into the inventory table.

```java
import java.sql.*;

public class InventoryManager {
    private static final String URL = "jdbc:mysql://localhost:3306/inventory_db";
    private static final String USER = "root"; // Default username for MySQL
    private static final String PASSWORD = "password"; // Replace with your password
```

```java
public static void main(String[] args) {
    try {
        // Load MySQL JDBC Driver
        Class.forName("com.mysql.cj.jdbc.Driver");

        // Establish the connection
        Connection conn = DriverManager.getConnection(URL,
USER, PASSWORD);

        // Create a statement
        Statement stmt = conn.createStatement();

        // SQL query to insert data into the inventory table
        String sql = "INSERT INTO inventory (name, quantity,
price) VALUES ('Laptop', 50, 799.99)";

        // Execute the query
        int rowsAffected = stmt.executeUpdate(sql);
        System.out.println("Rows affected: " + rowsAffected);

        // Close the connection
        stmt.close();
        conn.close();
    } catch (ClassNotFoundException | SQLException e) {
        e.printStackTrace();
```

```
    }
  }
}
```

This code:

- Loads the MySQL JDBC driver.

- Connects to the database.

- Executes an INSERT SQL query to add a product to the inventory.

3.2 Read Operation (SELECT)

Now let's retrieve all items from the inventory table.

```
import java.sql. *;

public class InventoryManager {
    private static final String URL =
"jdbc:mysql://localhost:3306/inventory_db";
    private static final String USER = "root";
    private static final String PASSWORD = "password";

    public static void main(String[] args) {
        try {
            // Load MySQL JDBC Driver
            Class.forName("com.mysql.cj.jdbc.Driver");

            // Establish the connection
```

```
    Connection conn = DriverManager.getConnection(URL,
USER, PASSWORD);


    // Create a statement
    Statement stmt = conn.createStatement();


    // SQL query to select data from the inventory table
    String sql = "SELECT * FROM inventory";
    ResultSet rs = stmt.executeQuery(sql);


    // Process the result set
    while (rs.next()) {
        int id = rs.getInt("id");
        String name = rs.getString("name");
        int quantity = rs.getInt("quantity");
        double price = rs.getDouble("price");


        System.out.println("ID: " + id + ", Name: " + name + ",
Quantity: " + quantity + ", Price: " + price);
    }


    // Close the connection
    rs.close();
    stmt.close();
    conn.close();
} catch (ClassNotFoundException | SQLException e) {
```

```
            e.printStackTrace();
        }
    }
}
```

This code:

- Retrieves all items in the inventory.
- Loops through the ResultSet to display each item's details.

3.3 Update Operation (UPDATE)

Let's update the quantity of a product in the inventory.

```java
import java.sql.*;

public class InventoryManager {
    private static final String URL = "jdbc:mysql://localhost:3306/inventory_db";
    private static final String USER = "root";
    private static final String PASSWORD = "password";

    public static void main(String[] args) {
        try {
            // Load MySQL JDBC Driver
            Class.forName("com.mysql.cj.jdbc.Driver");

            // Establish the connection
            Connection conn = DriverManager.getConnection(URL, USER, PASSWORD);
```

```
// Create a statement
Statement stmt = conn.createStatement();


// SQL query to update data in the inventory table
String sql = "UPDATE inventory SET quantity = 60
WHERE name = 'Laptop'";


// Execute the update query
int rowsAffected = stmt.executeUpdate(sql);
System.out.println("Rows affected: " + rowsAffected);


// Close the connection
stmt.close();
conn.close();
} catch (ClassNotFoundException | SQLException e) {
e.printStackTrace();
}
}
}
```

This code:

- Updates the quantity of the item "Laptop" in the inventory table.

3.4 Delete Operation (DELETE)

Finally, let's delete an item from the inventory.

```java
import java.sql.*;


public class InventoryManager {
    private static final String URL = "jdbc:mysql://localhost:3306/inventory_db";
    private static final String USER = "root";
    private static final String PASSWORD = "password";

    public static void main(String[] args) {
        try {
            // Load MySQL JDBC Driver
            Class.forName("com.mysql.cj.jdbc.Driver");

            // Establish the connection
            Connection conn = DriverManager.getConnection(URL, USER, PASSWORD);

            // Create a statement
            Statement stmt = conn.createStatement();

            // SQL query to delete data from the inventory table
            String sql = "DELETE FROM inventory WHERE name = 'Laptop'";
```

```
// Execute the delete query
int rowsAffected = stmt.executeUpdate(sql);
System.out.println("Rows affected: " + rowsAffected);

// Close the connection
stmt.close();
conn.close();
} catch (ClassNotFoundException | SQLException e) {
    e.printStackTrace();
}
}
}
```

This code:

- Deletes the item "Laptop" from the inventory table.

---

4. Hands-On Example: Build a Simple Inventory Management System

Now that we've covered the basics of JDBC and CRUD operations, let's create an **Inventory Management System**.

This system will allow users to:

- Add inventory items.
- View all items.
- Update item quantities.
- Delete items.

We've already discussed the CRUD operations in separate examples, but now let's combine them into a single class to manage the inventory.

Conclusion

In this chapter, we introduced you to **JDBC (Java Database Connectivity)** and how to use it to interact with relational databases in Java. We covered the following topics:

- **Setting up JDBC** and connecting to MySQL.

- Performing **CRUD operations** (Create, Read, Update, Delete) on a database using JDBC.

- Building a **Simple Inventory Management System** using JDBC to interact with the database.

By now, you should be comfortable with the basics of database interaction in Java, and you should be able to build more complex systems involving databases. JDBC is a powerful tool for building data-driven applications, and mastering it will help you create scalable and maintainable software.

Next Steps:

- Experiment with **prepared statements** for better security when working with user input.

- Add more features to the inventory system, such as sorting and searching items.

- Explore more advanced database features like **transactions, joins**, and **stored procedures**.

Now that you have a solid understanding of JDBC, you can create robust applications that integrate seamlessly with databases!

Chapter 13: Multithreading and Concurrency

Introduction to Multithreading and Concurrency

In today's fast-paced world, speed and efficiency are crucial in software development. As applications grow in complexity, managing tasks concurrently—i.e., executing multiple tasks simultaneously—becomes an essential technique. In Java, this is achieved through **multithreading**.

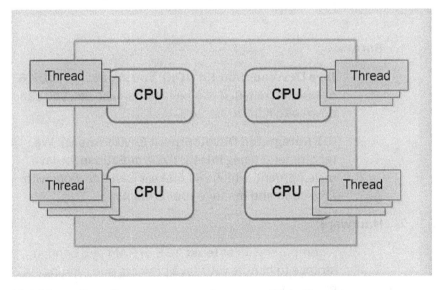

Multithreading allows a program to run multiple threads concurrently, enabling better resource utilization and performance. For example, tasks like reading data from multiple files or downloading multiple files can be performed simultaneously, significantly speeding up the overall process.

This chapter will explore the concept of **multithreading and concurrency** in Java, how to manage threads, and how multithreading can be used to improve the performance of data processing systems. We will build a **simple file downloader** application to demonstrate multithreading in action and explore how concurrency can be applied to real-world scenarios.

What You'll Need

Before diving into multithreading and concurrency, ensure you have the following setup:

1. **Software:**

   o **Java Development Kit (JDK):** You should have **JDK 8 or later** installed. If you haven't done so yet, you can download it from Oracle's website.

   o **IDE (Integrated Development Environment):** We recommend using **IntelliJ IDEA** or **Eclipse** for Java development, which will make it easier to work with Java code and manage your projects.

2. **Hardware:**

   o A computer with **at least 2GB of RAM** and enough storage to handle your Java projects and running programs.

3. **Prerequisites:**

   o Basic knowledge of **Java programming** (variables, control flow, classes, methods).

o   Familiarity with concepts like **objects, inheritance,** and **exception handling**. If you've followed the earlier chapters, you're ready to start with multithreading.

1. What is Multithreading?

Multithreading is a Java feature that allows multiple threads to run concurrently within a single program. A **thread** is the smallest unit of execution within a program. By using threads, a program can perform multiple tasks at the same time, making better use of system resources.

1.1 The Concept of Concurrency

Concurrency refers to the ability of a program to execute multiple tasks in overlapping periods. These tasks may not necessarily run simultaneously, but they progress in overlapping phases, giving the illusion of simultaneous execution. This is where **multithreading** comes into play: by dividing tasks into smaller threads, you can efficiently utilize your CPU and handle multiple operations concurrently.

1.2 Threads in Java

Java provides built-in support for multithreading. You can create a thread in Java in two ways:

1.   **Extending the Thread class.**

2.   **Implementing the Runnable interface.**

In both cases, the thread can be started using the start() method, and the run() method contains the code that will be executed by the thread.

2. Threads and the Runnable Interface

2.1 Extending the Thread Class

In Java, the Thread class represents a thread of execution. To create a custom thread, you can subclass the Thread class and override the run() method.

Example: Using the Thread class

```java
class MyThread extends Thread {
    @Override
    public void run() {
        for (int i = 0; i < 5; i++) {
            System.out.println("Thread running: " + i);
            try {
                Thread.sleep(500); // Pauses for 500 milliseconds
            } catch (InterruptedException e) {
                System.out.println(e);
            }
        }
    }

    public static void main(String[] args) {
        MyThread thread = new MyThread();
        thread.start(); // Starts the thread
    }
}
```

In this example:

- The run() method contains the task that will be executed when the thread is started.

- The Thread.sleep(500) pauses the thread for 500 milliseconds between iterations.

2.2 Implementing the Runnable Interface

Alternatively, you can implement the Runnable interface, which is more flexible since your class can inherit from other classes as well.

Example: Using the Runnable interface

```
class MyRunnable implements Runnable {
  @Override
  public void run() {
    for (int i = 0; i < 5; i++) {
      System.out.println("Runnable thread running: " + i);
      try {
        Thread.sleep(500); // Pauses for 500 milliseconds
      } catch (InterruptedException e) {
        System.out.println(e);
      }
    }
  }

  public static void main(String[] args) {
    MyRunnable runnable = new MyRunnable();
    Thread thread = new Thread(runnable);
    thread.start(); // Starts the thread
  }
}
```

/

In this example:

- The MyRunnable class implements Runnable and overrides the run() method.

- The Thread object is created with the Runnable instance and then started.

Both methods allow for the creation of separate threads of execution, enabling concurrency in your Java application.

---

3. Managing Threads with Executor Service

While creating individual threads using Thread or Runnable is fine for small applications, as your application grows and needs to manage multiple threads, it becomes cumbersome. This is where the **ExecutorService** comes in. The ExecutorService provides a higher-level replacement for the Thread class and allows you to manage a pool of threads efficiently.

3.1 What is ExecutorService?

ExecutorService is part of the **java.util.concurrent** package and allows you to manage a pool of worker threads. Instead of manually creating and managing threads, you submit tasks to the executor, and it takes care of the rest.

- **ThreadPoolExecutor** is a common implementation of ExecutorService and manages a pool of worker threads.

- The **ExecutorService** makes it easier to manage multiple tasks concurrently without manually handling thread creation and lifecycle management.

3.2 Example: Using ExecutorService

Here's a simple example where we use the ExecutorService to manage a pool of threads that perform a task concurrently.

```java
import java.util.concurrent.*;

class MyTask implements Runnable {
    @Override
    public void run() {
        System.out.println("Task is being executed by: " +
Thread.currentThread().getName());
    }
}


public class ExecutorServiceExample {
    public static void main(String[] args) {
        // Create a thread pool with 3 threads
        ExecutorService executorService =
Executors.newFixedThreadPool(3);

        // Submit 5 tasks to the thread pool
        for (int i = 0; i < 5; i++) {
            executorService.submit(new MyTask());
        }

        // Shut down the executor after all tasks are completed
        executorService.shutdown();
    }
}
```

In this example:

- We create a thread pool with 3 threads using Executors.newFixedThreadPool(3).

- We submit 5 tasks to the executor, and the tasks are executed by the threads in the pool.

- The shutdown() method is called after all tasks are submitted to properly shut down the executor service.

3.3 Types of Executors

1. **Fixed Thread Pool** (newFixedThreadPool): Creates a pool of fixed-size threads.

2. **Cached Thread Pool** (newCachedThreadPool): Creates a pool of threads that are created as needed and reused when available.

3. **Single Thread Executor** (newSingleThreadExecutor): Creates a pool with a single thread, ensuring tasks are executed sequentially.

---

4. Hands-On Example: Build a Simple File Downloader

Now that you understand how to manage threads, let's build a simple **file downloader** that uses **multithreading** to download multiple files concurrently.

4.1 Set Up the Downloader

We'll use the **ExecutorService** to manage a pool of threads that will download files concurrently.

Step 1: Create the FileDownloader class

```
import java.io.*;

import java.net.*;

import java.util.concurrent.*;
```

```
class FileDownloader implements Runnable {
    private String fileURL;
    private String destinationPath;

    public FileDownloader(String fileURL, String destinationPath) {
        this.fileURL = fileURL;
        this.destinationPath = destinationPath;
    }

    @Override
    public void run() {
        try {
            URL url = new URL(fileURL);
            try (InputStream in = url.openStream(); FileOutputStream out = new FileOutputStream(destinationPath)) {
                byte[] buffer = new byte[1024];
                int bytesRead;
                while ((bytesRead = in.read(buffer)) != -1) {
                    out.write(buffer, 0, bytesRead);
                }
                System.out.println("Downloaded: " + destinationPath);
            }
        } catch (IOException e) {
            System.out.println("Error downloading " + fileURL + ": " + e.getMessage());
```

```
        }
      }
    }


public class FileDownloaderApp {
    public static void main(String[] args) {
        ExecutorService executorService =
Executors.newFixedThreadPool(3); // Pool of 3 threads

        // List of files to download
        String[] files = {
            "https://example.com/file1.jpg",
            "https://example.com/file2.jpg",
            "https://example.com/file3.jpg"
        };

        // Submit tasks to download the files
        for (int i = 0; i < files.length; i++) {
            String destinationPath = "file" + (i + 1) + ".jpg";
            executorService.submit(new FileDownloader(files[i],
destinationPath));
        }

        // Shutdown the executor service
        executorService.shutdown();
    }
```

}

Explanation:

- **FileDownloader** implements Runnable and defines the run() method, which contains the logic for downloading a file.

- **ExecutorService** is used to manage a pool of threads (in this case, 3 threads) that download files concurrently.

---

5. Real-World Application: Enhancing Performance in Data Processing Systems

Multithreading can significantly improve performance, especially in large-scale data processing systems. Consider a system where you need to process large volumes of data, such as reading and processing log files, performing database queries, or handling multiple user requests.

5.1 Example: Parallel Data Processing

Imagine you have a large collection of records to process. You can use multithreading to divide the task into smaller chunks and process them concurrently, reducing the overall time required.

```
class DataProcessor implements Runnable {

    private int start;
    private int end;

    public DataProcessor(int start, int end) {
        this.start = start;
        this.end = end;
    }
```

```java
@Override
public void run() {
    for (int i = start; i < end; i++) {
        // Simulate processing data
        System.out.println("Processing data: " + i);
        try {
            Thread.sleep(100); // Simulate time-consuming task
        } catch (InterruptedException e) {
            System.out.println(e.getMessage());
        }
    }
}
}


public class DataProcessingApp {
    public static void main(String[] args) {
        ExecutorService executorService =
Executors.newFixedThreadPool(4); // 4 threads for processing

        int totalRecords = 100;
        int recordsPerThread = totalRecords / 4;

        // Divide work into 4 tasks and process concurrently
        for (int i = 0; i < 4; i++) {
            int start = i * recordsPerThread;
```

```
    int end = (i + 1) * recordsPerThread;

    executorService.submit(new DataProcessor(start, end));

  }


    executorService.shutdown();

  }
}
```

This example divides the total records into 4 parts and processes them concurrently using 4 threads, making the process faster.

---

6. Conclusion

In this chapter, we introduced **multithreading and concurrency** in Java. We covered:

- The concept of **multithreading** and how to create threads using the Thread class and the Runnable interface.

- How to manage a pool of threads with **ExecutorService** to improve efficiency in concurrent tasks.

- A **hands-on example** where we built a **file downloader** using multithreading to download multiple files concurrently.

- How **multithreading** can be applied to real-world applications like **data processing systems** to improve performance and scalability.

Chapter 14: Preparing for Java Interviews

Introduction

The world of software development is both exciting and competitive, and one of the most important steps in securing a role is succeeding in a **technical interview**. Whether you are a seasoned developer or just starting out, interview preparation is critical to your success. In this chapter, we'll focus on preparing you for **Java-related interviews**.

We'll cover **key Java concepts** you need to master before your interview, walk through **mock interview questions**, and help you develop effective **problem-solving strategies**. In addition, we'll tackle a **hands-on challenge** where you can apply these concepts and strategies to a real coding problem, just like you would in an actual interview.

By the end of this chapter, you will be well-prepared to tackle Java interviews confidently and efficiently, with the skills and mindset to solve algorithmic challenges.

What You'll Need

Before we dive into interview preparation, ensure you have the following setup:

1. **Software:**

   o **Java Development Kit (JDK):** You should have **JDK 8 or later** installed on your computer. If you haven't installed it yet, download it from Oracle's website.

- ○ **IDE (Integrated Development Environment):** We recommend using **IntelliJ IDEA** or **Eclipse** for Java development. These IDEs provide helpful features like syntax highlighting, auto-completion, and debugging tools.

2. **Hardware:**

   - ○ A computer with **at least 2GB of RAM** and sufficient storage to run Java projects and applications.

3. **Prerequisites:**

   - ○ Basic understanding of **Java syntax, OOP principles,** and **data structures.**

   - ○ A willingness to practice solving coding problems and prepare for interview-style questions.

---

1. Common Java Interview Topics

Before diving into interview questions, it's important to review the **key concepts** that are frequently tested in Java interviews. These concepts will form the foundation of your preparation.

1.1 Object-Oriented Programming (OOP) Principles

Java is an object-oriented language, meaning understanding **OOP principles** is essential for your interview. Here are the key OOP concepts that you should master:

1. **Encapsulation:** The practice of bundling data (variables) and methods that operate on the data into a single unit, i.e., a class. It also involves restricting direct access to some of the object's components, which can be done using access modifiers (private, protected, public).

2. **Inheritance:** A mechanism where one class can inherit fields and methods from another. This promotes code reusability

and the creation of hierarchical relationships between classes.

3. **Polymorphism**: The ability of a method, class, or object to take on multiple forms. In Java, polymorphism is commonly achieved through method overriding (runtime polymorphism) and method overloading (compile-time polymorphism).

4. **Abstraction**: The concept of hiding the complex implementation details and showing only the necessary features of an object. This can be achieved using abstract classes and interfaces.

1.2 Data Structures and Algorithms

Another key area of Java interviews is your understanding of **data structures** and **algorithms**. You should be comfortable with:

- **Arrays** and **Lists** (e.g., ArrayList, LinkedList)

- **Stacks** and **Queues**

- **Trees** (e.g., binary trees, binary search trees)

- **Graphs**

- **Hashing** (e.g., HashMap, HashSet)

- **Sorting** and **Searching** algorithms (e.g., QuickSort, MergeSort, Binary Search)

- **Recursion** and **Dynamic Programming**

Understanding the **time complexity** of different operations (Big O notation) is essential for solving algorithmic problems efficiently.

1.3 Java Syntax and Core Libraries

You'll also be tested on **Java syntax** and the core Java libraries. Key areas to focus on include:

- Java **collections** (e.g., List, Set, Map)

- **Exceptions** and **Error handling**

- **Java Streams** for working with collections in a functional programming style

- **Concurrency** and **multithreading**

- **File I/O** (Input/Output operations)

---

2. Mock Interview Questions

Let's walk through some common Java interview questions that test the concepts mentioned above. These questions will help you practice your knowledge of Java while preparing for the interview.

2.1 Question 1: Reverse a String

Problem: Write a Java program that reverses a string without using built-in functions like reverse().

Solution:

```java
public class ReverseString {
    public static String reverse(String str) {
        String reversed = "";
        for (int i = str.length() - 1; i >= 0; i--) {
            reversed += str.charAt(i);
        }
        return reversed;
    }

    public static void main(String[] args) {
        String input = "hello";
        System.out.println("Reversed string: " + reverse(input));
    }
```

}

- **Explanation:** We use a **for loop** to iterate over the string in reverse order and build the reversed string.

2.2 Question 2: Find the Factorial of a Number (Recursion)

Problem: Write a Java program to find the factorial of a number using recursion.

Solution:

```
public class Factorial {
    public static int factorial(int n) {
        if (n == 0) {
            return 1;
        }
        return n * factorial(n - 1);
    }

    public static void main(String[] args) {
        int number = 5;
        System.out.println("Factorial of " + number + " is: " +
factorial(number));
    }
}
```

- **Explanation:** The base case is when n == 0, where the factorial is 1. Otherwise, we recursively multiply n by the factorial of n-1.

2.3 Question 3: Check if a Number is Prime

Problem: Write a Java program that checks if a given number is prime.

Solution:

```
public class PrimeCheck {
    public static boolean isPrime(int num) {
        if (num <= 1) return false;
        for (int i = 2; i <= Math.sqrt(num); i++) {
            if (num % i == 0) return false;
        }
        return true;
    }

    public static void main(String[] args) {
        int number = 11;
        System.out.println(number + " is prime: " + isPrime(number));
    }
}
```

- **Explanation:** The method iterates through numbers from 2 to the square root of num. If num is divisible by any of these numbers, it's not prime.

---

3. Problem-Solving Strategies

During an interview, how you approach a problem is just as important as finding the right solution. Here are some problem-solving strategies to keep in mind:

3.1 Understand the Problem

Before jumping into code, **understand** the problem:

- Read the problem statement carefully.

- Clarify any ambiguities by asking questions (e.g., "Are negative numbers allowed?" or "What is the expected output?").

- Identify the inputs and expected outputs.

3.2 Break the Problem Into Smaller Pieces

Decompose the problem into manageable parts. Tackle each part individually before combining them into the final solution. For example:

- **Input validation**: Are there edge cases to consider (e.g., empty inputs, null values)?

- **Algorithm choice**: Which algorithm suits the problem best? Does it involve sorting, searching, or recursion?

3.3 Write Pseudocode or Plan Your Approach

Before writing the code, it's often helpful to write pseudocode or outline your approach. This gives you a roadmap to follow and ensures that you don't miss important steps.

3.4 Write the Code and Test Incrementally

Start coding the solution step by step:

- Write one part of the solution, then test it.

- Test edge cases and handle exceptions as you go.

- Refactor your code as needed, aiming for clarity and simplicity.

3.5 Optimize the Solution

Once your solution is working, ask yourself:

- Can the time complexity be improved?

- Can the space complexity be reduced?

For example, could you use **dynamic programming** to optimize recursive solutions? Or perhaps a more efficient algorithm (like **merge sort** instead of **bubble sort**) could be used?

---

4. Hands-On Challenge: Solve a Coding Problem in Java

Let's work through a coding problem together. The challenge is to implement a **Basic Inventory Management System** that can perform the following operations:

- Add a new item (product name, quantity, and price).

- Update the quantity of an existing item.

- Display all items in the inventory.

We'll use **Java collections** to store the inventory and implement the necessary CRUD operations.

Step 1: Define the Inventory Class

```java
import java.util.*;

class Item {
    String name;
    int quantity;
    double price;

    public Item(String name, int quantity, double price) {
        this.name = name;
        this.quantity = quantity;
        this.price = price;
```

```java
    }


    @Override
    public String toString() {
        return "Item[name=" + name + ", quantity=" + quantity + ", price=" + price + "]";
    }
}


public class InventoryManager {
    private Map<String, Item> inventory = new HashMap<>();

    // Add a new item
    public void addItem(String name, int quantity, double price) {
        inventory.put(name, new Item(name, quantity, price));
    }


    // Update an existing item
    public void updateItem(String name, int quantity) {
        Item item = inventory.get(name);
        if (item != null) {
            item.quantity = quantity;
        } else {
            System.out.println("Item not found");
        }
    }
```

```java
// Display all items
public void displayInventory() {
    for (Item item : inventory.values()) {
        System.out.println(item);
    }
}

public static void main(String[] args) {
    InventoryManager manager = new InventoryManager();

    // Add some items
    manager.addItem("Laptop", 10, 1200.00);
    manager.addItem("Smartphone", 25, 600.00);
    manager.addItem("Tablet", 15, 450.00);

    // Display inventory
    System.out.println("Inventory:");
    manager.displayInventory();

    // Update an item
    manager.updateItem("Laptop", 20);

    // Display updated inventory
    System.out.println("Updated Inventory:");
```

```
manager.displayInventory();
    }
}
```

Step 2: Explanation of Code

1. **Item class**: Represents an individual product with a name, quantity, and price.

2. **InventoryManager class**: Manages the inventory using a HashMap. It provides methods for adding, updating, and displaying items.

3. **Main method**: Adds items to the inventory, updates one of them, and displays the inventory before and after the update.

5. Conclusion

In this chapter, we explored the fundamentals of preparing for **Java interviews**. We covered:

- Key Java concepts to master before interviews, including **OOP principles, data structures**, and **algorithms**.

- Real-world interview questions and their solutions, focusing on Java syntax, problem-solving, and algorithmic thinking.

- Effective **problem-solving strategies** to help you approach coding challenges confidently.

- A hands-on challenge where we built a **Basic Inventory Management System** and practiced implementing common CRUD operations in Java.

By practicing these topics and solving problems on your own, you'll be better prepared for your next Java interview. Remember, **consistency** is key when it comes to interview prep. Keep solving problems, refining your solutions, and reviewing key concepts. Good luck, and happy coding!

Chapter 15: Real-World Java Projects

Introduction

In this chapter, we'll dive into some real-world Java projects that help you apply your skills and build useful applications that can solve problems in everyday life or business scenarios. By the end of this chapter, you will have practical experience in building several projects that include personal finance trackers, web applications with Spring Boot, full-stack development, and deploying applications to the cloud.

Through each project, we will walk you through the **entire process**— from project setup to the final deployment—while emphasizing the most important concepts, technologies, and best practices you'll need to know as you build real-world applications in Java.

What You'll Need

Before we start building, make sure you have the following setup:

1. **Software:**

   o **Java Development Kit (JDK):** You should have **JDK 8 or later** installed on your computer. If not, download it from Oracle's website.

   o **Spring Boot:** For building web applications, you will need **Spring Boot**, which simplifies Java web development. Spring Boot's documentation is a great resource for getting started, and you can install it from here.

- o **IDE (Integrated Development Environment):** We recommend using **IntelliJ IDEA** or **Eclipse** for Java development, as they both provide excellent support for Java, Spring Boot, and other related technologies.

- o **Database:** You will need a **MySQL** or **PostgreSQL** database to store and manage data for your projects. You can download MySQL from here, or PostgreSQL from here.

- o **Cloud Platforms:** To deploy your Java applications to the cloud, you will need accounts on **AWS** (Amazon Web Services) or **Heroku**. Both platforms provide tutorials on how to deploy Java applications.

2. **Hardware:**

- o A computer with **at least 4GB of RAM** and sufficient storage to run Java applications, databases, and cloud-deployed systems.

3. **Prerequisites:**

- o **Basic Java programming skills:** You should already know the fundamentals of Java, including OOP principles, Java syntax, and core libraries.

- o Familiarity with **web development concepts** and **databases** (SQL queries, relational databases).

- o An understanding of **HTTP, REST APIs,** and basic **front-end technologies** (HTML, CSS, JavaScript) for full-stack development.

1. Building a Personal Finance Tracker

Managing personal finances can be a hassle. This project is all about building a **Personal Finance Tracker** to track your income and expenses, generate reports, and store data in a database.

1.1 Features of the Personal Finance Tracker

The goal of this project is to create a simple app where users can:

- **Add income and expenses**: The user can log their income and expenses, including categories (e.g., groceries, rent, salary).

- **View reports**: The app will show an overview of income and expenses and provide summaries for different time periods.

- **Store data in a database**: Use JDBC or an ORM framework like **Hibernate** to store user data in a database (e.g., MySQL).

1.2 Setting Up the Project

Let's start by creating a simple **Maven** project in **IntelliJ IDEA**. This will manage the dependencies for the project.

pom.xml (Maven configuration):

```xml
<dependencies>
    <dependency>
        <groupId>org.springframework.boot</groupId>
        <artifactId>spring-boot-starter-data-jpa</artifactId>
    </dependency>
    <dependency>
        <groupId>org.springframework.boot</groupId>
        <artifactId>spring-boot-starter-web</artifactId>
    </dependency>
    <dependency>
        <groupId>mysql</groupId>
        <artifactId>mysql-connector-java</artifactId>
    </dependency>
```

</dependencies>

application.properties *(Database connection):*

spring.datasource.url=jdbc:mysql://localhost:3306/finance_db

spring.datasource.username=root

spring.datasource.password=password

spring.jpa.hibernate.ddl-auto=update

spring.datasource.driver-class-name=com.mysql.cj.jdbc.Driver

1.3 Creating the Database and Table

Create a database called finance_db in MySQL, then define a transactions table:

CREATE DATABASE finance_db;

USE finance_db;

CREATE TABLE transactions (
  id INT AUTO_INCREMENT PRIMARY KEY,
  description VARCHAR(255),
  amount DECIMAL(10, 2),
  type VARCHAR(50),
  date TIMESTAMP DEFAULT CURRENT_TIMESTAMP
);

Here, the transactions table has columns for description, amount, type (income or expense), and date.

1.4 Implementing the Backend

We'll now implement the backend using **Spring Boot** and **JPA** (Java Persistence API) to interact with the database.

Transaction Entity (Java class):

```java
import javax.persistence.*;
import java.math.BigDecimal;
import java.time.LocalDateTime;


@Entity
public class Transaction {

    @Id
    @GeneratedValue(strategy = GenerationType.IDENTITY)
    private Long id;
    private String description;
    private BigDecimal amount;
    private String type;
    private LocalDateTime date;

    // Getters and setters
}
```

Transaction Repository:

```java
import org.springframework.data.jpa.repository.JpaRepository;


public interface TransactionRepository extends
JpaRepository<Transaction, Long> {
```

}

Transaction Service:

```
import org.springframework.beans.factory.annotation.Autowired;
import org.springframework.stereotype.Service;

import java.util.List;

@Service
public class TransactionService {

    @Autowired
    private TransactionRepository transactionRepository;

    public void addTransaction(Transaction transaction) {
        transactionRepository.save(transaction);
    }

    public List<Transaction> getAllTransactions() {
        return transactionRepository.findAll();
    }

    public List<Transaction> getTransactionsByType(String type) {
        return transactionRepository.findByType(type);
    }
}
```

1.5 Building the Front-End (Web Interface)

Let's create a simple **HTML form** for adding transactions and displaying them.

index.html:

```
<!DOCTYPE html>
<html lang="en">
<head>
    <meta charset="UTF-8">
    <meta name="viewport" content="width=device-width, initial-scale=1.0">
    <title>Personal Finance Tracker</title>
</head>
<body>
    <h1>Personal Finance Tracker</h1>
    <form action="/addTransaction" method="POST">
        <label for="description">Description:</label>
        <input type="text" id="description" name="description"><br><br>

        <label for="amount">Amount:</label>
        <input type="number" id="amount" name="amount"><br><br>

        <label for="type">Type (Income/Expense):</label>
        <select id="type" name="type">
            <option value="income">Income</option>
```

```
<option value="expense">Expense</option>
</select><br><br>

<input type="submit" value="Add Transaction">
</form>

<h2>All Transactions</h2>
<ul id="transactions">
    <!-- Transactions will be listed here -->
</ul>
</body>
</html>
```

2. Web Application with Spring Boot

Now, let's dive into creating a **CRUD web application** with **Spring Boot.** We will build a simple **REST API** to interact with our database and a basic **front-end** to interact with users.

2.1 Setting Up Spring Boot

We've already set up the pom.xml with Spring Boot dependencies in the finance tracker project, so we'll continue from there.

To create a **REST API,** we will add **Controller** classes to handle HTTP requests.

2.2 Creating a REST API

TransactionController:

```
import org.springframework.beans.factory.annotation.Autowired;
```

```java
import org.springframework.web.bind.annotation.*;

import java.util.List;

@RestController
@RequestMapping("/transactions")
public class TransactionController {

    @Autowired
    private TransactionService transactionService;

    @PostMapping("/add")
    public void addTransaction(@RequestBody Transaction transaction) {
        transactionService.addTransaction(transaction);
    }

    @GetMapping("/all")
    public List<Transaction> getAllTransactions() {
        return transactionService.getAllTransactions();
    }

    @GetMapping("/{type}")
    public List<Transaction> getTransactionsByType(@PathVariable String type) {
        return transactionService.getTransactionsByType(type);
```

```
    }
}
```

2.3 Running the Application

To run the Spring Boot application, use the command:

mvn spring-boot:run

Now, the app should be accessible at http://localhost:8080. You can use Postman or any HTTP client to test the API by adding transactions and retrieving them.

3. Deploying Your Java Applications

Once you've built your Java application, it's time to deploy it so others can access it. In this section, we'll go over how to deploy your **Spring Boot** application to cloud platforms like **AWS** and **Heroku**.

3.1 Deploying on Heroku

Heroku is one of the easiest platforms to deploy Java applications. Here's how to deploy a Spring Boot app to Heroku.

1. **Install the Heroku CLI**: Follow the instructions here.

2. **Create a Heroku Application**:

3. heroku create my-java-app

4. **Deploy the Application**:

5. git push heroku master

6. **Open Your Application**:

7. heroku open

Your Spring Boot application is now live!

3.2 Deploying on AWS

For AWS, you can deploy Java applications using **Elastic Beanstalk**.

1. **Install the AWS Elastic Beanstalk CLI**: Follow the instructions here.

2. **Initialize Your Application**:

3. eb init

4. **Create an Environment and Deploy**:

5. eb create

6. eb deploy

7. **Open the Application**:

8. eb open

Your app will now be available on AWS!

---

4. Building a Full-Stack Java Application

In this section, we will demonstrate how to build a **full-stack Java application**, integrating **Spring Boot (backend)** with a **front-end framework** like **React** or **Angular**.

4.1 Backend (Spring Boot) with REST API

The backend will be the same **Spring Boot application** we built earlier with CRUD operations exposed through RESTful endpoints.

4.2 Frontend (React) Setup

1. **Create a React App**:

2. npx create-react-app finance-tracker-frontend

3. **Install Axios for HTTP Requests**:

4. npm install axios

5. **React Code**: Inside App.js, fetch the list of transactions from the backend and display them:

```jsx
import React, { useState, useEffect } from 'react';
import axios from 'axios';

function App() {
  const [transactions, setTransactions] = useState([]);

  useEffect(() => {
    axios.get('http://localhost:8080/transactions/all')
      .then(response => {
        setTransactions(response.data);
    });
  }, []);

  return (
    <div className="App">
      <h1>Personal Finance Tracker</h1>
      <ul>
        {transactions.map(transaction => (
          <li key={transaction.id}>{transaction.description}:
${transaction.amount}</li>
        ))}
      </ul>
    </div>
```

```
  );
}
```

export default App;

4.3 Connecting Frontend and Backend

Once the backend is running, you can **start the React frontend** by running:

npm start

The React app will fetch data from the Spring Boot API and display it dynamically on the frontend.

---

5. Conclusion

In this chapter, we built several **real-world Java projects**:

- A **Personal Finance Tracker** using Spring Boot and a MySQL database.

- A **CRUD web application** with **Spring Boot** and **REST APIs**.

- A **full-stack Java application** with **React** and **Spring Boot**.

We also covered how to **deploy Java applications** to platforms like **Heroku** and **AWS**.

These projects will give you the practical experience needed to work with **Spring Boot, databases,** and **front-end technologies,** as well as the know-how to deploy applications to the cloud. With these skills, you're now prepared to take on real-world Java development challenges!

Next Steps:

- Explore **security** (e.g., authentication, authorization) in your Java web applications.

- Try integrating **advanced features** like user authentication, file uploads, or payment gateways into your applications.

www.ingramcontent.com/pod-product-compliance
Lightning Source LLC
Chambersburg PA
CBHW070947050326
40689CB00014B/3372